Adam and *Steve*

Adam and Steve

The Rules for Men Attracted to Other Men

Russell Baptist, LCSW

Copyright © 2019 by Russell Baptist, LCSW.

All rights reserved. No part of this publication may be reproduced, distributed, or transmitted in any form or by any means, including photocopying, recording, or other electronic or mechanical methods, without the prior written permission of the publisher, except in the case of brief quotations embodied in critical reviews and certain other noncommercial uses permitted by copyright law. For permission requests, write to the publisher, addressed "Attention: Permissions Coordinator," at the address below.

Scripture quotations marked KJV are from the Holy Bible, King James Version (Authorized Version). First published in 1611. Quoted from the KJV Classic Reference Bible, © 1983 by The Zondervan Corporation.

Scripture quotations marked NIV are taken from the *Holy Bible, New International Version. NIV.* © 1973, 1978, 1984 by International Bible Society. Used by permission of Zondervan. All rights reserved. [Biblica]

ARPress
45 Dan Road Suite 36
Canton MA 02021

Hotline: 1(800) 220-7660
Fax: 1(855) 752-6001

Ordering Information:
Quantity sales. Special discounts are available on quantity purchases by corporations, associations, and others. For details, contact the publisher at the address above.

Printed in the United States of America.

ISBN-13:   Paperback   979-8-89389-410-3
           eBook   979-8-89389-411-0

Library of Congress Control Number: 2024916562

In memory of my great-aunt Bloneva "Eva" Spells, whose spirit always guided me no matter where I found myself in life, and for all those same-sex-attracted men who cannot speak for themselves.

Contents

Acknowledgments xi
Preface xiii
The MAM Anthem (We) xvii
Introduction xix

The Rules on MAM Maturity Status 1
- The Neophyte Stage 3
- On Mannerisms 5
- The Family Members' Role 7
- Bullying 9
- On Personality 11
- The Ingénue Stage 15
- On Maturity 17
- The Supernova Stage 21
- The Ikonoclass Stage 24
- The Legacy Stage 28
- When the Stages Interact 32

The Rules for Good Living and Your Power 35
- From MAM to Heterosexual 37
- From MAM to Heterosexual 39
- On Your Truth 43
- On Talent 46
- On Anger 49
- On Coming Out 53
- On Being Defined By Who You Sleep With 56
- On Greatness 59

- How to Get What You Deserve 62
- You and Your Circle of Friends 65

The Rules on Style, Intimacy, and Making a Connection 69
- On Style, Beating Your Mug, and Affectation 71
- In Your Villa and Holding Court 77
- On Reading, Shade, Trade, and on the Low 80
- On Being Crafty 95
- On Getting in Them: Drags and Trannys 97
- What Is a MITCH, Bisexuality, MCM, and Understanding the Maydar Factor 101
- The Relationship Components, Marriage, and When Love Leaves 110
- Online Activity, Cruising, the Rambles, Tea Rooms, and Person to Person 120
- On Pastimes and Athleticisms 129

The Rules on Sex and Sexuality 138
- The Penis a.k.a. Your Johnson 140
- Fellatio a.k.a. Giving Head 146
- The Gluteus Maximus a.k.a. The Booty 150
- Analingus or Tossing Salad 154
- Intercourse 101 156
- Definition of Top, Bottom, and Versatile 159
- Frottage 166
- Three-Ways, Orgies, and Sex Parties 171
- S&M, Raw Sex, and Breeding 175
- Sexually Transmitted Diseases (STDs) 180

The Rules on History and the Bible, the Torah, and the Quran 193
- Nature's Scheme 195
- On Genetics 198
- Mankind and the Circle of Life 201
- Jonathan and David 204
- Prehistory and Other Cultures 209
- Christianity: The Beginnings 212
- God, Abraham, and Sin 214

- Genesis and Acts of Violence...218
- Leviticus and Questions Raised...220
- Paul's Real Mission, Worldview, and the Word Effeminate....223

The RAB Rules a.k.a. the 800 Series...229
Verbal Erotic Management..240
The Rules in Texts and Tweets..243
The MAM Anthem (I) 251

Acknowledgments

There have been many mentors, colleagues, staff, even friends and family who over the years have contributed to my understanding and development of this book. I have to first acknowledge the thousands of individuals, clients, and workshop participants over these years that contributed to my knowledge base. Anyone who has achieved some sort of success in their careers started with family. I have the best of families, including Warren and Elmira Bass, my grandparents who raised me to be the best at my chosen path. To my mother Elizabeth, my brothers William and Darryl, and my dear sister Vanessa, your love and support overwhelm me. I must include my aunts, uncles, nephews, nieces, and cousins, namely Antoinette, Kimberly, Melinda, Johnnie, and Sean ; the family's mutual love is unconditional. And to Thomas Bess, words cannot express my appreciation for your influence, guidance, and love. Lorraine, Viola, and Russell, you are very special to me.

While the Bronx, New York City, is my birthplace, my roots and foundation come from Palm Beach County, Florida. I acknowledge the Palm Beach Gardens High School Class of 1975: You were the first who made it comfortable for me to be me. To my lifelong friends and family, namely Phillip and Shairette, Stephanie, and Vincent (RSVP)—all of you taught me confidence through your love. Along my journey, my political worldview was shaped by my educational foundation and other cultural experiences at Texas College in Tyler, Texas. It was my Washington DC experience that shaped my adulthood.

Thank you, Janet, my big sister, for lifting me when I could not do it for myself. Where would I be without the graduate-level education I obtained at the august Columbia University and the School of Social Work? The Center for Urban Community (CUCS) made my professional bona fides and this book possible. Unity Fellowship Church helped me connect with my spirit and provided me with an understanding about the role of religion. Gay Men of African Descent (GMAD) helped me connect to the community on both local and national levels.

Thank you to the village of Harlem for the rich history of my neighborhood, the Hill, and to the great friends I have today, you know who you are. Also, I carry with me the eternal flame of the ancestors and peers who have passed on through my life.

A special appreciation for you, the reader; words cannot express what it means to me that you decided to spend your time experiencing what my book has to offer.

Preface

A few years ago, I was sitting in my back room, settling down for my evening of MSNBC and/or CNN. It was just another night for me anticipating the latest fact-free assault on Pres. Barack Obama by conservative pendants. Since my freshman year in college when we helped elect Jimmy Carter to the U.S. presidency, I have enjoyed engaging in politics through the media and by exercising my right to vote. Reading the *New York Times*, the *Huffington Post, Time* magazine, and other online media for political news is a pastime for me. A few years ago, it seemed to me that stories about teenage suicides began to take center stage in the media. For example: *Eleven-year-old Jaheem Herrera woke up April 16 acting strangely. He wasn't hungry, and he didn't want to go to school. But the outgoing fifth grader packed his bag and went to school at Dunaire Elementary School in DeKalb County, Georgia. He came home much happier than when he left in the morning, smiling as he handed his mother, Masika Bermudez, a glowing report card full of As and Bs. She gave him a high-five, and he went upstairs to his room as she prepared dinner. A little later, when his little sister called him to come down to eat, Jaheem didn't answer. So the mother and the daughter climbed the stairs to Jaheem's room and opened the door. Jaheem was hanging by his belt in the closet. "I always used to see these things on TV, dead people on the news," says Bermudez. "I saw somebody die and to see the dead person is your son. Hanging there, a young boy . . ., to hang yourself like that, you've got to be tired of something."*

Bermudez says bullies at school pushed Jaheem over the edge. He complained about being called gay, ugly, and "the virgin" because he was from the Virgin Islands, she said. He used to say, *"Mom, they keep telling me this . . . this gay, gay word. I'm tired of hearing it. They're telling me the same thing over and over,"* she told CNN as she wiped tears away from her face (Mallory Simon, CNN 2010).

Jaheem was not alone; a fifteen-year-old named Billy Lucas from Greensburg, Indiana, hanged himself in his family's barn. In California, a young teenager named Seth Walsh hanged himself in the family's backyard.

Asher Brown, from Texas, barely a teenager, shot himself in the head. Then there was the case of eighteen-year-old Tyler Clementi, the Rutgers University freshman, who jumped off the George Washington Bridge in New York City after being confronted about his sexuality.

These untimely deaths made headlines in media like the *New York Times*, local papers, cable TV, and popular social media platforms . It was the first time that America was able to really open its eyes to what many young males who are attracted to the same sex experience at some point in their early adolescent development. America was able to authentically grieve for those five most unique individuals and their families who loved them. I thought to myself that these five teenagers may have ended their lives, but to me, they are heroes. Their deaths shone a bright light on the many thousands of adolescent males who have also taken their lives in silence. Only their families were left with the grief, guilt, and trauma; their stories will never be told. Why did these teenagers feel so alone? As a mental health professional, I knew the factors that contribute to suicide in teenagers, and one big contributor is bullying. It made me think about how many more attempt to, or have to die because there are no positive same-sex role models within their environment. Who will say to them that they did not have to live in fear because they act or look different from males in their age group? More importantly, who will help support and educate the parents, guardians, or family members about the life of male same-sex attraction.

Adam and Steve: The Rules for Men Who Are Attracted to Other Men (MAM) was written to address a number of aspects concerning male same-sex attraction. The rules are a mixture of fact-based evidence and anecdotal informational experiences I collected over many years of interviews with MAMs. This book reflects my conversations with same-sex-attracted men through my travels in rural towns and urban areas, including states like New York, Georgia, California, Texas, North Carolina, Florida, and Washington DC.

If you are a teenage male struggling with your sexual identity, then you will learn you are not alone and that your life matters. If you are an adult MAM, then the rules will be a reminder of what you already lived through and your responsibility to those males growing up behind you. If you are a heterosexual family member reading this book, then you will have a few tools to provide support to your son, brother, uncle, cousin, or even your father. After reading the rules, you should walk away with a sense of curiosity and freedom knowing that you are armed with a little more information about male same-sex attraction. Information leads to power and knowledge, which will help to intellectually defend ourselves and others like us when the opportunity presents..

Russell A. Baptist, LCSW
New York, New York

Men Who Are Attracted to Other Men

The MAM Anthem (We)

We are quicksilver, a fleeting shadow, and a distant sound;
Our home has no boundaries beyond which we cannot pass;
We live in a flash of color, in music, in fashion, in finance, in sports, and in the great works of art;
We live on the wind, in the sparkle of a star; we are his children; and we are her children, the chosen ones;
We are the men who are attracted to other men!

Edited by: Russell Baptist

Introduction

Why do you need *Adam and Steve: The Rules for Men Who Are Attracted to Other Men (MAM)?* The rules say the answer to that question is "why not?" We are living in a young new century, and like never before, cultural issues that affect MAMs are a part of the world's conversation. Gays in the military, marriage equality, DOMA, in other words the basic right to live your MAM lives with the freedoms afforded to most heterosexual people. Travel around the United States or any other free society and you may see a small percentage of people who are attracted to the same sex in positions of influence and power. But you will also see many of them, out of the closet or not, who do not feel free to be themselves. During the printing of this book, while acceptance of same sex marriage is on the rise, more than 50 percent of people in the United States consider same-sex attraction morally acceptable. Currently, several sports figures have come out to the public, and even popular national team sports are addressing the issue. Despite this acceptance, LGBTQ people remain fearful about living their lives out loud and abundantly. The reason for this fear could be that within the USA today, in more than half of the states, you can be fired by your employer because you are attracted to the same sex. Moreover, there are around thirty-nine states with laws on the books that support transgender, drag queen, and transsexual bias. These state laws prove that the United States has a long way to go to achieve same-sex equality.

Many conservatives believe that God speaks with them and only them. Armed with this misinformation, their stance is to purport that only Adam and Eve can have divine grace. In turn, Adam and Steve, and Ana and Eve exist because of bad or evil influences in today's society.

The religious right's political power holds your career in their hands. If you are in the public eye, they will not allow many of you to come out because of their influence on Q-ratings or music sales or sports contacts or an acting career. How many MAM teenagers have been asked to leave their parent's or guardian's home because of their same-sex attraction? Some argue that this homophobic influence from the religious right is passed down from generation to generation. As a result of this family lineage, bullies are born. These are the boys who ridiculed some of you emotionally and/or physically when you were a young child because somehow he suspected you were different. Most MAMs are able to grow through the trauma of bullying, but sadly, there are many who do not. As of 2010, in the USA, only about eight states have laws on the books declaring that it is illegal to harass someone because of sexual orientation. Something has to change. Many same-sex attracted teenagers experience physical violence, verbal abuse, social isolation, and sexual harassment. These circumstances were in the forefront of this author's mind when this book was conceived. One of the goals in writing the rules is to help break the cycle of hopelessness. Deaths by suicide highlight the need to really address the millions of same-sex attracted teen or preteen who are being bullied at the hands of peers as well as some adults.

Each chapter of the rules for the most part is written in the second person. In other wordsone of the objectives in the book is to speak to you, the reader.

While reading the rules another goal is that many of you understand how to apply them in your life. Also, you must question what you read and be prepared to add your own experiences to the topics covered in this edition of *Adam and Steve: The Rules for Men Who Are Attracted to Other Men (MAM)*. In this book, there will only be very few passing references to the word *gay*. Many will agree that the word *gay* is about to become passé, and some argue that it does not reflect the true diversity of individual same-sex behavior. Not all MAMs express themselves in identical ways, andthere's a spectrum that should be acknowledged and recognized.

The rules are divided into five chapters. Each chapter contains ten rules that are labeled under what is called a series. When discussing male same-sex attraction as its own culture, included are the stages of development. Contained within the maturity status or the MS rules is a view of the five generational stages of development, the rites of male passage in time. The five stages of same-sex maturity are introduced: the neophyte, the ingénue, the supernova, the ikonoclass, and the legacy stages. What stage do you fall under?

Next the reader discovers good living, and your power or the GLP rules takes you on a self-efficacy journey. These rules provide you with a road map about your place in this world, the uniqueness of who you are as told through the eyes of historical MAM pioneers.

In the chapter on style, intimacy, and making a connection, the SIMC rules discuss swagger, attitude, sex appeal, and how your entire physical appearance is key. Contained within these rules is a spectrum of behavior within the community, and you will find out why a one-size description does not fit all.

Sex and sexuality, or the SS rules, cover the male sexual anatomy, sexual activity, safe sex options, and risky behaviors.

The last ten rules have to do with history, including the Bible, the Torah, and the Quran, in other words the HBTQ rules. These rules will provide you with counterarguments concerning biblical books in Genesis, Leviticus, Romans, Timothy, and Corinthians. The religious right uses the major biblical books to postulate their belief that same-sex attraction is somehow against God.

Next, you will find writings covering what is called the RAB rules a.k.a. the 800 series. This chapter was written to address issues that the previous ones did not cover. The final chapter provides you with all fifty rules in texts and tweets! It gives the reader an opportunity to send the messages learned in the book through social media to a worldwide audience. The rules begin and end with the MAM anthem. The anthem part one is for the collective we and the last is for the personal I. The anthem is designed to end any public gathering of men who are attracted to the same sex.

Let's get started.

The Rules on MAM Maturity Status
The MS Rules 300–310

Before you begin your journey about where you fall within the stages of maturity, or the MS Rules series 300–310, the author would like to remind you of the goals of *Adam and Steve: The Rules for Men Who Are Attracted to Other Men*. This book, along with its rules, was written to establish that a same-sex-attracted male culture exists. This culture has its own customs, norms, beliefs, and language. MAMs has its own social, intellectual, and artistic expressions, no matter your identified race, familiar community, or ethnic background. The contents of the book speak to basically three audiences:

The teen or preteen male struggling with sexual identity will learn that he is not alone and that his life matters.

The adult MAM will be reminded of what he's already lived through and his responsibility to those same-sex-attracted males who are younger.

The heterosexual family member reading this book will have a few tools to provide support to a son, brother, uncle, cousin, or even a father. With that said, enjoy the experience beginning with the MS rules.

The rules identify the behavioral and developmental components of many same-sex-attracted males called the five stages of maturity. They are the neophyte stage, the ingénue stage, the supernova stage, the ikonoclass stage (not to be confused with iconoclast), and the legacy stage.

The neophyte stage happens long before adolescence until the late teens and, for some, the early twenties. The term *neophyte* comes from the Greek word which means new, beginning, or an awakening. One feature of this stage is that you are experiencing a very unconscious learned behavior that helps identify who you will become as a mature person. The adults in your life must be supportive of who you are becoming. They should not attempt to enforce their gender and cultural bias to try to change your behavior. Family members have a role in your development, and these influences can be positive or negative. What family members should realize is that your actions are predisposed and mostly influenced by a chemical called testosterone. This well-known chemical not only controls male growth and development, but it also affects emotional reactions no matter your sexuality.

Then there is the ingénue stage, which happens when you are approaching young adulthood until around the early thirties. The term *ingénue* is a French word used to describe a young adult who is newly arrived on the scene or screen for public view; it means an innocent.

Although this stage is filled with learning experiences, both smooth and rocky, in the ingénue stage, these experiences will only help you become ready to take on the task as an emotionally healthy supernova and beyond.

The supernova stage occurs between the ages of about thirty-three to around forty-six years old. When you reach this stage in life, you have made a past for yourself. Now you will begin to reap the rewards of lessons learned. In other words, good or bad, you burn brightly in both your professional and your personal life.

At about the age of forty-seven to around sixty-three years old, you have achieved what the rules call the ikonoclass stage. In the world of MAMs, when you've reached this stage, you are now in a rarefied category that denotes wisdom, experience, and power. It is the ikonoclass who helped paved the way for neophytes, ingénues, and supernovas to have the small freedoms they have today.

In addition to the ikonoclass stage, the rules will introduce you to the legacy stage. If you are in the legacy stage, you may be as young as in your mid to late sixties or beyond. Legacy, more than any other stage, have had the most experience with change. The knowledge base of this stage is phenomenal; you are keepers of the flame. At the legacy stage, you are a sage, the custodian of wisdom. It is you who have the historic institutional knowledge that the other stages must recognize, appreciate, and celebrate.

The chapter ends with information about the responsibility of each stage when they interact with one another in public or private settings. With that said, here are the MS rules!

The Neophyte Stage
MS Rule 301

For men who are attracted to other men, maturity begins during the first realization of sexual awareness, which is called the neophyte stage. The term comes from the Greek word which means new, beginning, or just getting started. This stage happens before adolescence to around late teens, or for some, the early twenties. Research studies find that sexuality is developing when you enter puberty. In most cases, you are truly naïve about what it's really like to be attracted to the same sex. It is normal for you to keep your newfound sexual experimentations private. The myth is that most of you can be sexually influenced by an adult who is flamboyant, or gay images that can be seen in the media will make you mimic that behavior is simply not true. The facts are several well-respected studies have concluded that external influences have no bearing on same-sex attraction. For example, no amount of media exposure can teach you this life because same-sex attraction must be experienced. First, you should understand that this time is uncomfortable for all male children. One reason is that consequential thinking has not caught up with body growth. In other words you may be physically big as an adult but emotionally you're still a child. On top of that, you are carrying a same-sex secret. When this occurs, many neophytes seem to push limits and test adult authority just like any other teenager. This stage is not only confusing for the parents/guardians, but it is also especially difficult for you as the child who is attracted to the same sex. Neophytes are physically, socially, and emotionally stressed out.

The neophyte stage is a time for males to learn how to feel comfortable in their own skin; this is not an easy process for the individual.

It is the period when your life is being shaped by who you find to emulate. It could be other male family members, but often they are athletes, musicians, supermodels, or celebrities. Without knowing it, in your core, you attempt to take on their mannerisms. What is occurring at that time is that you are finding someone to identify with on the road to manhood. The mannerisms that are acquired are unconsciously learned behavior. Hang in there, as any adult will tell you growing up attracted to the same sex is a huge learning experience. Furthermore, it has a significant impact on your future development and behaviors as you mature.

The Neophyte Stage
MS Rule 301

What sentence(s) in this rule stands out for you?

How would you define this rule for your social media followers?

On Mannerisms
MS Rule 302

Within the neophyte stage, behaviors displayed through mannerisms tend to go from one end of the spectrum to the other. During this stage, you will express your mannerisms either subtlety, not drawing too much attention to yourself, or overtly, feeling so secure that you could be yourself publicly under any circumstances. In other words, in this stage, your mannerisms will either conform to what society views as acting masculine, or you may display feminine mannerisms. One thing for sure, in many cases, you try to adjust to who you are becoming. The majority will keep the new self-discovery a secret. This private same-sex exploration is not shared with parents and other family members.

Some in the early neophyte stage may become fascinated with their mothers' clothes. They may find an attraction to cartoon superheroes or a pro ball player, even GI Joe. This attraction could also extend to movie or pop culture celebrities, or you may become fascinated with the wardrobe or the hair of your sister's Barbie doll. Many times this and other influences can develop into sexual exploration with peers in the same age group.

At around age ten to twelve, your hormonal curiosity is peaked when unexplained erections and body hair development occur. It's the realization that, as a male, you have a unique sexual instrument. This is when you lock yourself in the bathroom and discover your "five-finger stroke motion"!

In the neophyte stage, some of you will become apprehensive yet aroused during events like shower time after a game or in the school gym locker room or when having sleepovers.

The neophytes' apprehension is tempered with excitement that comes from fear of possibly having an erection in front of other peers. A number of teenage boys will experience this attraction, even if briefly. The desire for a male to see how his own penis compares to others is overwhelming. This is also a stage when a small fraction, whether heterosexual or homosexual, will develop lifelong issues concerning a form of penis envy, wondering if your size is enough for your partner's sexual gratification.

On Mannerisms
MS Rule 302

What sentence(s) in this rule stands out for you?

How would you define this rule for your social media followers?

The Family Members' Role
MS Rule 303

The rules state that parents, guardians, and other family members must be supportive of the neophyte's self-expression or face the long-term consequences of doing nothing. It is dangerous when family attempts to enforce heterosexual gender/cultural values on him in this stage. Remember, nature cannot be changed by human intervention. Family members will witness self-expression displayed in many different ways depending on the individual's style and comfortably.

There are some who will express themselves by dressing extravagantly or perhaps making sure that every color matches from head to toe. There will be subtle clues like the way the hair is worn, cut, or colored. Some neophytes even try on makeup or wear clothing that society would judge should be worn by females.

Then there are other individuals who will exhibit none of the forms of self-expression described previously. This group tends to participate in athletics or other cultural norms for teenage males. He reveals self-expression by being purposely low key around the family and remaining under the radar. His life centers around activities that are totally male dominated like the boy scouts, team and individual sports; silence is how he chooses to self-express. As a family member, pay attention to the behavioral clues.

What does a same-sex-attracted youth want? He wants what every other young person wants—family love, family support, and security.

As a family member, love means not judging your child because of who he is becoming; listen to him without offering advice. Family should be supportive without smothering; make it safe by instilling in him cultural values without restricting his right to self-determination. What is not recommended in this stage is a family member's criticism or indifference. He should not hear preaching about how things used to be, nor should he hear assumptions about his possible sexual explorations. For example, phrases like *stop acting like a girl, or you're going to be a sissy boy* must be avoided. This is not a message a child should hear from family members. Try to avoid the question: do you have a girlfriend? If he had one, you would already know; you should not have to ask. Comparing him to other heterosexual male relatives should be avoided as well.

The Family Members' Role
MS Rule 303

What sentence(s) in this rule stands out for you?

How would you define this rule for your social media followers?

Bullying
MS Rule 303 B

This rule is particularly important when it comes to how the family and a neophyte respond to the traumatic experience of bullying. If bullying goes unchecked or is ignored, then negative consequences can happen. Trauma reveals itself when the neophyte becomes uninterested in school; he may even run away from home.

In addition, the changes in neophyte's behavior because of bullying, family indifference, or abuse can lead to other mental health issues like major depression or develop personality disorders. It is well known that depression is the leading cause of teenage suicide. When parents or other families observe signs or depression and suicide thoughts, a referral should be made to a mental health professional. If the teen will not seek assistance for suspected depression, then it is perfectly appropriate for the family to call emergency services.

One last thing about bullies, some teenage males who commit acts of bullying are themselves dealing with internal uncomfortable sexual feelings, peer pressure, and ignorance in many cases because of a lack of positive parental guidance.

Bullying
MS Rule 303 B

What sentence(s) in this rule stands out for you?

How would you define this rule for your social media followers?

On Personality
MS Rule 304

The neophyte stage is the time when you begin to shape your likes and dislikes according to your individual personality. During this period, not only does your voice deepen, pubic hairs appear, but along with erections, your curiosity kicks into high gear. There are several chemicals inside your body interacting with each other during this time. But the chemical called testosterone has a powerful influence on your personality traits.

Most adolescent males will have an overwhelming desire to become expressive. GI Joe and Barbie are over; trying on mother's clothes phase is gone. Playing cops and robbers or hide-and-seek are a thing of the past. It is the discovery that the innocence of the time prior to adolescences is complete. It's time to use your smart phone or to create a social media profile for rendezvous with other neophytes. In other words, the stakes are higher once a same sex male enters the late neophyte stage.

Most teenage males branch off into four categories; either they are heterosexual, homosexual, tranny, or bisexual. Let's look at bisexuality, the ability to find both genders erotically gratifying. In the neophyte stage, being bisexual is no indication that you will remain that way throughout adulthood. For example, you may mature into being attracted to only females, or you may just stay with males, or you may remain bisexual. A few of you in this stage will not act out sexually with another male, but you do think about what it's like.

As you mature, that thought can become a preoccupation or a curiosity, but you may never become physically intimate with males. This phenomenon is otherwise known as being bi-curious. However, there will be many who will explore what it's like to have intimate sexual relations with the same gender.

As a neophyte, you start to understand the importance of relationships outside the family unit. These relationships can have many forms and associations. One of these associations has to do with being a member of a house. A house, in its purest form, is made up of a group of same-sex-attracted males who have a special commonality. One commonality is that collectively the individual represent the artistic theme or style of each member.

A house is usually named after an international fashion icon or a locally famous MAM. Usually, the oldest members take on the role as the mother or the father of the house. Houses are important in the MAM community because it provides sense of family to neophytes who may not have had that kind of support in birth families or the school community. As a member of a house, participating in vogue contest, runway modeling, and face competitions is what you live for!

Winning trophies, cash prizes, and community recognition are all a part of what happens in a ball. A ball usually occurs four times a year, each season. These events provide many young adult MAMs with an opportunity to showcase their dancing, costume designing, and theatrical talents. Houses not only allow neophytes to use new talents, but more importantly, being a member helps build lasting interpersonal relationships with like-minded individuals who are mostly peers.

There are others during the neophyte stage that will excel in team and individual sports like basketball, football, baseball, swimming, or running track. The athletic neophyte in some cases plays significant leadership roles in extracurricular activities and individual sports. While you're seen as a leader, you work hard to balance heterosexual conversations about dating girls for fear of being exposed or judged. Intellectually, there are some teenagers who will use this stage to great advantage like going to college or becoming an apprentice at a vocation or enlisting in the armed forces. Many in this stage are just figuring it all out; the path is laid out for you. Take advantage!

Then there are other neophytes who will publicly express MAM personality by wearing female attire like the so-called fem queens or as a drag queen or transvestite (tranny). In this stage, there are a small group of some same-sex-attracted males who publicly indentify as straight with a different kind of secret. These men become what the rules call a MITCH; this subset can only live out their bisexual fantasies by exclusively engaging in relationships with drag queens or transvestites who look like actual females, (more about both groups in a later chapter).

A great gift most teenage males will receive in this stage is that you will gain an Aunt Haggy. She can best be described as a heterosexual female or even asister/friend who understands you. She knows your personality and most of your secrets. She will defend you in front of anyone, and you can get her to follow wherever you go in your small town or big city. Aunt Haggy loves you unconditionally; some call these females fag hags or beards, but the rules call them affectionately Aunt Haggy. Some in the public assume she's your girlfriend, and the two of you rarely confirm or deny this theory. Even after the neophyte stage, throughout your lifetime, there will always be an Aunt Haggy around. As a MAM, you will love her like family; it is platonic, it is real, and it is just the rules!

Overall, this stage is about finding out about who you are, what you want, what you are comfortable with, and what turns you on.

On Personality
MS Rule 304

What sentence(s) in this rule stands out for you?

How would you define this rule for your social media followers?

The Ingénue Stage
MS Rule 305

The ingénue stage begins at around age eighteen and ends during the early thirties. The term *ingénue* is a French word used to describe an adult who is young and new with little experience. It means you just arrived on the scene for the public to view; it identifies you as an innocent. When you're an ingénue, what you lack in life experience. You make up for it in every other way. This stage is like being ripe, low-hanging fruit. Three things can happen to low hanging fruit:

It falls to the ground. It is picked up and eaten by him because it has a great flavor.

It does not fall but is taken off the tree, but because it's not yet ripe, he throws the fruit away.

It falls to the ground but left on its own; it grows into a beautiful, strong big tree.

The fruit analogy describes the ingénue stage perfectly. Life as a brand-new adult MAM is just starting. The world, unlike it was in the neophyte stage, is all of sudden your oyster. By now, you have either graduated from college, or you are going through college. Some of you may be employed on your first job or making a name for yourself artistically. The point is, you are using this stage to figure out your personal journey. Ingénues are, as they say, the belle of the ball or the last bottle of water in the desert. This stage is the peak time in a MAM's life when you are in possession of ethereal beauty; your body is defining itself, and your face, as they say, is sitting perfectly. But be careful; this physical handsomeness can be your blessing as well as your cruse!

During this time, you are sought after and admired no matter what body type you may possess. Youth is a weapon; knowing your worth in this stage helps you understand and recognize your own power as a blossoming adult MAM. When it comes to a conquest or a love interest, you feel like all sexual desires are attainable. In your mind, you can have who you want and when you want him. There will be many ingénues who will not realize their power; if this is you, then your learning experiences may take a little longer to grasp, but fear not. You will!

The Ingénue Stage
MS Rule 305

What sentence(s) in this rule stands out for you?

How would you define this rule for your social media followers?

On Maturity
Rule 306

In the ingénue stage, you are continuing your experiment with adult life. In other words, you are legally authorized to be responsible for the actions you take in your personal journey. This is the time, in theory, when you are supposed to begin to actualize what it means to be mature. In this stage, you ask yourself:

Where do I go from here?

What kind of mature adult will I become in my thirties and beyond?

How will I shape my destiny?

Many ingénues, unless independently wealthy, will work hard and attempt to take the world by storm. Some of you may have limited financial resources, may be living from paycheck to paycheck, may be staying with family, or may have a roommate. There are a few of you who may use your physical attractiveness to make money in the sex trade. Sex for money can be described broadly as getting into pornography or hustling or receiving monetary gifts from someone usually older.

The good thing about this behavior is that in most cases, making money from the sex trade is time limited; as you age, sex for money becomes more difficult. The bad thing about this activity, besides risky sex, is recording what you do on the Internet. In other words, exhibitionism is your right, but Web site video or going viral may come back to haunt you at a time when you least expect it. The rules say be cautious and consider the consequences of your actions; make positive decisions.

Ingénue's are old enough to discover MAM pastimes like going to clubs and bars. For some, the weekend can begin as early as Wednesday evening. Each night brings a new experience as you discover what best suits your tastes.

In clubs and bars, you learn about what kind of liquor, wine, or beer you enjoy or not. There are those of you who will experiment with legal and illegal drugs. Substances first used in the ingénue stage include marijuana or Cannabis sativa. Trees or exotic is one of the more popular psychoactive substances mostly used in a recreational way. While smoking weed has not been proven harmful to human physiology, man-made pharmaceuticals are far more dangerous. These pharmaceuticals include circuit drugs like GHB or G otherwise known as gamma hydroxybutyrate. GHB affects your central nervous system.

Then there's MDMA, mollies, e-pills, or ecstasy; these drugs provide you with extreme pleasure while distorting time and perception along with disruptions in your motor skills.

Last but not least, there is the notorious party-n-play drug called methamphetamine a.k.a. crystal meth. Some say crystal is pleasurable because it releases sexual inhibitions. However, the effects of crystal are devastating, causing an extreme change in appearance, emotional disturbance, including becoming susceptible to HIV and other STDs.

Heroin, cocaine, and sometimes crack cocaine can all be a part of the ingénue experience as well. Before you consider psychoactive substances, know the facts its up to you.. Substance use has the potential to ruin your life, and it can cause your young career to come to a crashing halt. Rules covering substance use issues are included in later chapters.

On a lighter note, in the ingénue stage, as you become a member of the MAM community, a sense of being a part of something outside of yourself is realized. This is the time when you began to formulate your own circle friends made up of other MAMs who have the same things in common as you do. Even taking on a lover becomes real for you at this stage. The length of time you and a lover(s) are together can be as short as a few weeks or several months or even as long as a few years. No matter the length of time, the experiences with a lover(s) will never be forgotten as you grow throughout the life stages. As an ingénue, you will more than likely take your first trip out of town.

In the spring, cities like Philadelphia, Washington DC, South Florida beaches, including Puerto Rico are fairly reasonable and attractive.

New York City, Fire Island, the Hamptons, and Seattle are good early pride summer excursions. Cities such as Austin, Los Angeles, San Francisco, Chicago, and Vegas can put a smile on your face as well.

In the fall, you may find yourself traveling to places like The Dominican Republic, Atlanta, Key West, or P-Town.

During the season of lent, the caravels in places like Trinidad, Brazil's eastern coast, Havana, and New Orleans become hot destinations for MAMs to gather.

European places of interest like the Greek Isles, Barcelona, Amsterdam, and the French Riviera can be great first-time destinations for you as well.

On the other hand, you can create your own new destination for the community to enjoy. The point is men attracted to the same sex men in this stage will explore either one or many of these points of interest. Although this period is filled with learning experiences, both smooth and rocky, these experiences will only help you become ready to take on the task as an emotionally healthy supernova.

On Maturity
Rule 306

What sentence(s) in this rule stands out for you?

How would you define this rule for your social media followers?

The Supernova Stage
MS Rule 307

The supernova stage occurs around the age of thirty-three to about forty-six years old. In this stage, by now you have made a past for yourself. There have been a few peaks and valleys in your life; it's time to benefit from lessons learned. In other words, as a supernova, you burn brightly, and you are ready to climb life's ladder. By now, you realize that the time has come for you to get serious about who you are and what direction you are headed. At this point, you are taking the action steps toward your personal and professional goals. During the supernova stage, you are creating your own personal history. Now you are a fully formed adult becoming a strong, maturing MAM. When you become a supernova, you are no longer the youngest person in the room, at the party, in the office, or even in college.

If you have biological children or you are raising children, they are becoming old enough to ask questions about your sexuality. Even other family members may have questions as well. The family's way of coping with the unknown is allowing you the right time to confirm or deny your same-sex attraction. Remember, do not allow children and other family to force you to make a pronouncement about who you are; the choice is yours and so is the timetable.

As a supernova, you become comfortable enough to settle into a long-term interpersonal relationship. By now you know what stimulates you about another male's spirit and his anatomy. More importantly, by now you should know how to articulate what turns you. If you belong to a house or another social organization, then you are now a role model. The younger MAMs should come to you for advice and guidance.

Going to clubs, bars, and parties remain an important part of your life instead of starting the party in the middle of the week; partying begins on Friday nights and ends on Sunday. When you do go out, you stick with your close circle of family/friends (CFFs). Then there are some supernovas that will have gym memberships or become captain of the championship sports team or score the most points in a game. If you are drag queen or transvestite/tranny, you are now one of the masters. Your mug (face) has been beaten for points with paint and powder; no one can clock you! The cash prizes for ballroom runway or for lip-sync contests are yours to win.

As a supernova, your physical appearance in most cases has perfectly matured; your chest is pumped, and your body is in peak condition. In other words, your look is flawless. By now, not only do the ingénues adore you; but in this stage, you are also sought after by the ikonoclass and preferred by the legacies. This is the time in your life when you have traveled to many of the MAM's out-of-town destinations. During these years, you know which destinations are more to your liking. In other words, you don't need a special event to travel to these places.

If you are a supernova today, then you grew up during the time of the HIV/AIDS crisis and the widespread substance use explosion during the 1980s and 1990s. Therefore, it can be enticing for some MAMs in this stage to think about participating in the risky behavior that resulted in sexually transmitted diseases and substance use of that time.

Then again, some of you will be tempted to take illegal steroid-based drugs to accelerate muscle development. Critical thinking is a must when faced with these decisions. The stakes are higher because in this stage, you have more to lose, like your health, career, and future retirement benefits.

As a supernova, you enter the job market in a serious way; this is the time to plant professional roots. Understanding job politics is critical for your specialized growth and development. Once you land the job, you should begin to learn who is in your corner and the colleagues who are not. Your work ethic will need to speak for itself. Coworkers and managers alike should begin to see you as a leader who knows how to be a team player. The time has arrived for you to take advantage of every opportunity to capitalize on your skills and positive reputation. With each promotion, your professional profile rises higher and higher in your chosen field. Supernovas begin to understand the value of paying off student loans, using health care, and establishing bank accounts. By now you are purchasing your own adult car, and/or you no longer just have a place to stay, but you make it a home. All of these activities prepare you to set in motion the leap from supernova to the ikonoclass stage.

The Supernova Stage
MS Rule 307

What sentence(s) in this rule stands out for you?

How would you define this rule for your social media followers?

The Ikonoclass Stage
MS Rule 308

The ikonoclass stage happens from about your late forties and ends around the early sixties. In the world of MAMs, you are now in a rarefied category that denotes wisdom, experience, and power. The bottom line is that you have been there and done that! As an ikonoclass, you paved the way for the neophyte, ingénue, and supernova stages to enjoy the fruits of your hard-fought struggles. Today there is recognition that you were able to organize others during the 1980s and 1990s, resulting in the creation of many iconic LGBTQ groups that exist today. In the professional arena, the ikonoclass in most cases are the presidents, CEOs, department directors, principles, and general managers; you lead others. If you are in the arts, then your career span decades; your authenticity and fame has been well established. Ikonoclass represents the gatekeepers, the possessor of the keys to the MAM kingdom. In this stage, it should be your responsibility to ensure that other qualified MAMs walk through the doors where you have power and influence. The learning experiences you have had in the previous three stages have made you an emotionally healthy advocate. Therefore, your history and knowledge should be passed down and kept alive.

The learning experiences that you can pass down are as simple as sharing your own special experiences, having gone through those earlier stages. Younger men attracted to the same sex will learn by your confidence and achievement that comes from ikonoclass' hard-fought struggles. Using the present day as an example, growing up in the late 1960s, 1970s, and 1980s were very different times. It was those decades that forged your principles, like respect for self, respect of privacy, and respect of others.

For instance, when you were a growing up, there was a sense of mystery concerning the pleasures and the pain of adulthood. The Sears and Montgomery Ward catalogs, comic book superheroes, and secret celebrity crushes were all you had to fantasize with during your pre-adolescence days. When you were a neophyte, for many, life was about living in the shadows of fear and shame. However, by the end of the 1970s, there were newly recognized civil rights, a young gay movement, and a form of music calleddisco..

For today's ikonoclass, early adulthood was full of possibilities and new discoveries. There were hardly any out MAM role models in the media, including politics or pop culture for that matter. To escape from several centuries of living in the shadows, dance music called disco sustained MAMs in the 1970s. This music brought heterosexual and homosexual people together without judgment; it gave you a platform to express yourself publicly. During those years, gay bars and discos from San Francisco to New York City to even the nation's capital provided gay men with a sense of belonging and camaraderie. While clubs and having a good time was a way of life for many men who are attracted to the same sex, coming out of the closet was rare.

Sexuality during the late 1970s and 1980s was mostly reduced to clandestine liaisons, places like bookstores, or twenty-five-cent peep shows, tea rooms, rambles, and the infamous bathhouses. Before there was cruising on the Internet and social media, MAMs found each other the old-fashioned way; you met him in person. Bookstores were places where some MAMs gathered to what appeared to be a magazine establishment. However, for twenty-five cents behind a beaded curtain, there were dark, low-lighted areas.

In those semidark places, you watched blurry Betamax pornographic movies. Those places provided several men who are attracted to the same sex with an opportunity to meet anonymously and have each other with no strings attached.

Some will argue that in addition to peep shows, bathhouses were the place to be. There you could take time to explore your sexual curiosity. Bathhouses had been a same-sex male institution since the fifteenth century. During the 1950s and through the 1980s, these institutions were mostly in big cities where mostly men attracted to the same sex pay for an entrance fee to be in a space with a steam room, a pool, and an anonymous entertainment. Included in the fee, you were able to rent either a small closet with enough room for him and you to stand up in with the door closed. On the other hand, you could rent a bigger version of the closet with a cot that stretched from wall to wall. There was always group action in the steam room, in the shower area, and in the pool. The concept of coming out was still relatively new; most MAMs lived their lives in the secret, even in big cities. Places like bars, discos, parks, peep shows, and bathhouses gave MAMs a new sense of sexual and personal freedom.

However at that time, no one knew that a health crisis of epidemic proportion was about to emerge. Ikonoclass witnessed the last days' sexual freedom but was also there when the very first cases of HIV/AIDS occurred in the USA. The first AIDS cases were discovered in San Francisco and New York City in 1981. According to Avert, an International AIDS charity, during the mid to late 1980s up until the late 1990s,worldwide, more than eight million people, mostly men who are attracted to the same sex had either died or had been infected with the disease.

The HIV/AIDS epidemic changed the way MAMs interacted with each other sexually. This disease initiated the closing of bathhouses, along with other sexually promiscuous places; at almost the same time, disco music died as well. The struggles that occurred, starting in the 1980s, helped Ikonoclass channel that energy to fight for the causes like homophobia, HIV/AIDS, suicide, violence, and bigotry. The MAM community began to come out of shadows and realize a common public bond. Organizations like Parents and Families of Lesbians and Gays (PFLAG), the Human Rights Campaign (HRC), Gay Men's Health Crisis (GMHC), Gay Men of African Decent (GMAD), the Minority Task Force (MTF), and the Gay and Lesbian Alliance against Defamation (GLAAD), along with many other civil rights groups, were all created with assistance from your generation. These organizations are now more than thirty years old. Ikonoclass established nationwide pride festivities and assisted in the creation of LGBTQ centers across the country.

If you are living in this stage and you are in a relationship, then you have mastered the formula to keep each other interested. The sex in your relationship has evolved into an understanding that is deeper than any physical act. On the other hand, if you are single, then you are thinking about who should be anointed with your intimate time. As a matter of fact, the time you spend with a man sexually is based on what feels good to you. There are times when you may feel like being with just you because you now know how to enjoy your own company. In addition, you have learned how to triumph over the habit of instant gratification. As an ikonoclass, you have an internal direction that moves you gracefully forward into the legacy stage.

The Ikonoclass Stage
MS Rule 308

What sentence(s) in this rule stands out for you?

How would you define this rule for your social media followers?

The Legacy Stage
MS Rule 309

The legacy stage happens from around your midsixties and beyond. Unlike the pervious stages, it covers a wide range of generations. When you've reached this stage, you could be as young as a few years away from retirement or well into your seventies or eighties. Legacy, more than any other stage, has had the most experience with change. It's true; you really have a story to tell because you are the ultimate survivor in the world of MAMs. There is a serenity that only you can have because your same sex heritage speaks for itself. There are not many situations which are unfamiliar to you because you have pretty much seen it all. The strong character you possess is your hallmark; you have blazed trails, and you set the standard for how to live in dignity. When you become a legacy in theory, you should be finically stable enough to enjoy the lifestyle to which you've grown accustomed during your reclining years. By now, you have an appreciation for how to succeed during changing times. In this stage, you wear gray hair like nobility; it is an adornment that denotes your life experience.

To know what it's like to reach the legacy stage, all you have to do is speak with a MAM born before or during the late 1940s. This was a time when denying who you were, and living a closeted life was the norm. To be publicly accused of same sex behavior meant breaking the law.

Before the 1970s, if you were an adult MAM, then you had to be clever in your camouflage so that family, neighbors, and coworkers would not question your sexuality. The term *gay* had nothing to do with same-sex attraction; it meant a state of being representing happiness and living a carefree life. In a time before social networks and chat rooms, the only way you knew if someone was same-sex attracted was to ask certain code questions. The code questions were used in public to disguise what was then referred to as a love that dared not speak its name. One question often asked when you suspected that another MAM was in the room: introduce yourself and ask him, are you a friend of Dorothy? Then there are those who found out by directly asking: do you want to swing an *epp*?

The Dorothy question had to do with a movie called *The Wizard of Oz*, the fantasy about escaping to place where you could be yourself and no one judged you, somewhere over the rainbow. Swinging an *epp* referred to the act of having a mostly one-time sexual encounter with a bisexual or another male on the DL. After the hookup or sexual episode or epp, it was never spoken of again by either party. The term *top* or *bottom* did not exist back then. If you hooked up with another man, you needed to understand two choices. Is the guy you're about to sleep with a pitcher or a catcher? Back in those days, other codes included wearing a bandana on the left side of your pocket or the right side, and the same concept applied to the wearing of earrings. Other codes used to cover sexuality at that time included talking about your relationships in terms of the pronoun "they" or "them." The point was you had to go through elaborate means to hide from the world who you were inthose years.

Some legacies had arranged marriages to women or were married to them "in name only" because it was required by the cultural traditions at that time. Before the 1970s, most all-male bars were considered illegal by law and had to exist in secret. In several places, especially urban areas, these secret MAM bars were at times rumored to bemob-owned. The thinking back then was these establishments were a good way to clean illegal money. The police, many of whom were corrupt, would take a monetary cut of the profits just to look the other way. If you wanted to dress in drag or wear anything that was considered feminine, then you had to take your hair and makeup with you to dress up after you entered the bar. At the end of the night before you left the bar, you change from your club clothes to your socially acceptable ones before going back into the public. While the times were not easy, it created the balls and houses neophytes, Ingénues, and others enjoy today. Entertainment events like the famed Jewel Box Revue and Role Reversal shows ruled the day. These and other iconic events gave many men attracted to the same sex a shared sense of identity. In addition, these events provided the heterosexual public a peek into an aspect of the same-sex-attracted culture.

The biggest contribution of your generation today is the gift of same-sex acceptance and pride. In the late sixties, MAMs were swept up in the Black American struggle for civil rights and later the new women's movement as well. Toward the summer of June of 1969, things came to a boil. Several men attracted to the same sex around the country were mourning the death of the iconic Judy Garland. MAMs became fed up with hiding in the shadows that's when the now legacy generation took action.

Garland's famous song, "Somewhere over the Rainbow", became the rallying cry. That summer in New York City, a group of mostly Black American drag queens began fighting for your right to be who you are today. Their example started a series of protests and riots that shook the United States to its very core. The following year, pride parades were held in New York City, Los Angeles, and San Francisco; it happened in June 1970. The rainbow from that famous song became the colors of the movement, and the rest, as they say, is history!

The organization called ACT UP was created by several MAMs who are now in the legacy stage. ACT UP contribution to society is more than just HIV/AIDS recognition and demanding funding. But it was the way they conducted protest that has become the standard for what you see in today's acts of civil disobedience. If you are close to a legacy, then you are not only connected to the history of MAM culture; you are also connected to your future. Companionship is the hallmark of what some may deem important in this stage. Another important aspect of legacies is sharing lessons learned with those of you who are in the previous stages. As a community, the rules challenge all neophytes, ingénues, supernovas, and ikonoclass to befriend a MAM in the legacy stage. Adhering to this rule will give you knowledge you can use in your own longevity. Keep in mind: if you live long enough, it is a natural fact that one day you will become a legacy!

The Legacy Stage
MS Rule 309

What sentence(s) in this rule stands out for you?

How would you define this rule for your social media followers?

When the Stages Interact
MS Rule 310

As a reminder, there are five stages that represent MAM development and maturity. They are neophyte, ingénue, supernova, ikonoclass, and legacy. In most cases, as previously reviewed these stages have their distinct features; and no matter what generation you find yourself in, there is one thing you have in common, and that's a shared experience in time. However, there are moments when the stages may interact with each other. This can occur in several ways, from a supernova teaching a neophyte in a classroom to an ingénue employed by an ikonoclass or a legacy. All stages may interact on social media, at a celebration or during special events, or even in the bars. In many cities, there are bars and events that encourage bears and cubs parings. Some say the terms *bears* and *cubs* came out of the connections between the different generations.

When the interaction turns sexual, there are rules for all stages to follow. In most cases, each stage seeks sexual gratification by choosing their peers or someone within a few years of their age group. However, there are quite a few supernovas, ikonoclass, and legacies that look toward ingénues for sexual relationships or one-night stands or booty calls. There are many reasons why some men in the latter stages are attracted to young adults. The reasons vary from person to person, but a common thought is that young adults provide older MAMs with a real sense of sexual adrenaline. The truth is most of them feel like someone in their own age group cannot replace this rush.

There are also many young adults who are attracted to older men for either guidance or stability or to replace patriarchal family figures. The young adult may want someone older who could help them navigate through the MAM way of life. Many ingénues are not necessarily sexually attracted to the older male. It's more about the learning experience that the older adult provides. Another incentive that more mature MAMs provide to their younger counterparts is finical support. Pay-to-play is as old as mankind, and there is an understanding in this situation that money is provided in exchange for sex. No judgment should be rendered about this exchange as long as both parties are adults; it's frankly not your business. The obligation of the adult generations is if you cannot be a positive role model, then allow especially the neophytes to grow up and develop without your interference. If you are aware of an adult engaging in sexual relations with anyone under eighteen, then that person is in some states committing a crime. Engaging in sexual molestation with children under fourteen is called pedophilia. If a child is under in most states the age of seventeen, the adult could be guilty of sexual molestation or statutory rape. These acts are not only morally inappropriate, but the damage they cause to neophytes will have lasting effects well into adulthood. The effects of childhood sexual trauma can have a huge impact on male high school dropout rates, criminal behavior, adult mental health issues, including substance use and sexual addictions.

When the Stages Interact
MS Rule 310

What sentence(s) in this rule stands out for you?

How would you define this rule for your social media followers?

The Rules for Good Living and Your Power
GLP Rules 200-210

This series of rules concerns itself how to realize your vast strength, power, and influence. The first rule titled "From MAM to Heterosexual" answers the question: can someone or something change your same sex nature? In this chapter, the rules stimulate your curiosity from a psychological perspective. The GLP rules will explore the evolution of homosexuality through the lens of the medical community. The concept of conversion or reparative therapy is reviewed and debunked. Experimental reparative myths must be exposed because of all the damage that has been done to many MAMs over the years. These types of so-called therapy attempts to do this, all in the name of changing who you are. While the term *conversion therapy* is fairly new, the idea about turning someone from homosexual to heterosexual is not. A classic example of this is the woman who is aware the man she is attracted to is not heterosexual. This knowledge, however, does not deter her from thinking she can control his sexual attraction. In other words, having vaginal sex will make you become a "real man." Another example: for those of you who grew up in, say the apostolic, holiness, church of God, Mormons and even some Southern Baptists, you may have had the experience of social isolation, even temporary imprisonment designed to drive the homosexual out of you!

These extreme traumatizing experiences have one thing in common; none of them worked. It is a universal truth that your same sex biology is all nature, and it has nothing to do with your physical environment or how you were nurtured.

Living things on this earth are either plant or animal; each of these living organisms has a natural order that occurs without interruption.

The universal order plays itself out by allowing each plant and animal to coexist with each other and depend upon each other for their survival. The top animal for the last several thousand years on this planet is a minimal species known as mankind, the human race. Any sociologist will tell you that humans are the top species because of a large brain, and the human brain is hardwired to create tools and believe in a higher being. Humans grieve for the dead, adapt to and control their surroundings. Also, they create family and social bonds. However, many beliefs and cultural norms are learned behaviors, such as language, the arts, values, and laws. A majority of the research shows one thing is irrefutable: being same-sex attracted is not a learned behavior.

As you begin to understand your place in this world, the rules on good living and your power or the GLP 200 to 210 series is handed to you so that you can be inspired to live your life with abundance. Highlighted in most of the GLP rules are examples of MAM historical figures that lived in time when to be accused of same-sex attraction could mean imprisonment or death. These MAMs are pioneers whose lives will encourage you to own your authority and stand in the truth about who you are. The chapter also discusses how to use your talents as a way to help yourself and others, if you choose.

Included here, you will find out about how anger issues can affect your self-confidence and place limits on your success. In the GLP rules, you will answer questions about coming out and how not to be defined by who you sleep with. There is information in this chapter about shame and how it can be healed. Finally, the GLP series ends with inspirational stories concerning how to attain greatness and getting what you deserve. Let's do this!

From MAM to Heterosexual
GLP Rule 201

If something is a fact, then it has to be supported by evidence. Former Sen. Patrick Moynihan of New York once said, "You are entitled to your own opinions but not your own facts." Conversion theory or reparative therapy is the belief that religion, along with several forms of early psychoanalysis and behavior modification treatments, will help homosexuals and bisexuals turn into heterosexuals. If you are involved in reparative therapy, then it is assumed that you overidentified with your mother when you were a small child.

As the theory goes, the only way to correct this same-sex dysfunction is to be psychologically repaired! There are several different ways to be repaired or converted into heterosexuality or so they say. Let's look at a few: You must participate in contact sports; you must spend time with heterosexual men and imitate their behavior at sporting events and bars, including their affect; you must attend church or synagogue and join a men's group; you must avoid any social activities that are associated with homosexuals; you must engage in sexual intercourse with a woman, get married, and father a child.

When you have completed these practices, you have been repaired, and you are cured of homosexuality according to the proponents of this idea. No wonder every responsible professional organization, including the American Psychiatric Association, the American Psychological Association, the American Medical Association, and the National Association of Social Workers, all consider conversion/reparative therapy harmful, and it is not based in scientific evidence or fact.

In the early twentieth century, the father of psychoanalysis Sigmund Freud, as a part of the Oedipus complex, theorized that most boys between the ages of four and five wanted to have sex with their mothers. Freud's theory went on to state that boys believed that if their fathers found out about this desire, then their fathers would castrate them. In addition, the theory stated that it was at this time when boys begin to understand that they had only two choices in order to avoid castration. They could either identify with the father or become heterosexual, who would subconsciously sexualize his mother and replace her with other females.

On the other hand, these boys can go in another direction and become detached from the father. When this happens, boys do not subconsciously think about the mother as a sex object; they overidentify with her instead. In other words, the group of boys who overidentify with the mother will engage in same sex attraction.

While Sigmund Freud's theories about some aspects of psychoanalysts were not supported during later years, he was ahead of his time publicly stating his opinion that same-sex attraction was not a psychological disorder. When Dr. Freud penned his famous letter to an American mother in 1935, he wrote that same-sex attraction was difficult enough in society; it should never be considered an illness or pathology. He went on to say that same-sex-attracted people were no different than anyone else. He named well-known homosexuals in European history to illustrate their contributions to culture. Freud was in total disagreement with federal and state laws that treated homosexual activity as a crime or mental illness during his lifetime.

The labels homosexuality and bisexuality have had an interesting journey and a strange history in the mental health field. During the first half of the twentieth century, despite Freud's observations, homosexuality was defined as a mental disorder. As a matter of fact, it took evidence based empirical studies conducted by Dr. Alfred Kinsey in the late 1940s and important research by Dr. Evelyn Hooker, along with the gay rights movements, to change the medical view about same sex attraction.

Together, these outside realities at that time caused the American Psychiatric Association to remove homosexuality and bisexuality from the Diagnostic and Statistical Manual of Mental Disorders (DSM) as a mental illness.

Toward the end of the twentieth century, even the term *ego-dystonic homosexual* was taken out of the DSM altogether. Based on these facts, the notion that you are conditioned to same-sex attraction or someone else can "turn you out" or that being a MAM is mentally unhealthy is simply not true.

From MAM to Heterosexual
GLP Rule 201

What sentence(s) in this rule stands out for you?

How would you define this rule for your social media followers?

On Your Authority
GLP Rule 202

The definition of authority means that as a MAM, you are elite because you possess an expertise about your own power. This power is evidence by your responsibility toward other individuals, your relationship to the external environment, or how you interact with others and your chosen career. There are two main types of authority; one is known as vested authority and the other is called authentic authority. Vested authority happens when because of your expertise, you are quickly rewarded by the establishment where you are connected or where you work. In other words, vested authority must be conferred upon you by someone who is more powerful than you. Authentic authority means that your power is creditable, valid, and legitimate. It is not always officially given; it's innate, and everyone connected to you recognizes it. When you have authentic authority, you are genuine, and your leadership comes from a unique internal drive that can influence others around you. Now that you have a working definition, here are the questions: Is your authority vested, or is it authentic?

Can both of these concepts coexist within the same person?

Whose life can I look to as an authentic role model for me and other MAMs?

A good example of a role model is a MAM who, through his authentic authority, was able to influence history and move human rights forward around the world. Since he was a little boy before 1920, he knew he was attracted to other males. This teenager was so confident about who he was as a MAM that he came out as early as thirteen years old, decades before the concept of coming out existed! As a matter of fact, he was even confident during the time of Jim Crow segregation when laws existed that made homosexuality a crime in every state. Despite segregation and same-sex criminal laws, he decided to love for the sake of love—it did not matter if the man's race was black or white. His authentic authority made him a great man who was free in spirit. This man who is attracted to the same sex dated whom he wanted, even when, because of the color of his skin, he could not eat in the same restaurant as his lover; his authentic authority would not allow him to keep quiet about injustice. He was extremely tall, well dressed, and he had a sharp wit. This MAM would dedicate his life to fight for oppressed people everywhere. In the late 1930s, he learned nonviolent civil rights from the writings of Mahatma Gandhi. He worked with A. Phillip Randolph in the 1940s, playing a leadership role in helping the sleeping car porters unionized. This great MAM personally lobbied President Truman for racial equality in the United States. It is partly due to his efforts that segregation was eliminated from the U.S. military. His influence was worldwide; he worked to free India from British rule and helped to free South Africa from Dutch rule as well.

However, this great man's claim to fame was his profound influence over southern preacher named Martin Luther King Jr. It was he, not Dr. King, who conceptualized and helped organized the 1963 March on Washington. He taught Dr. King the principles of nonviolence, and he gave Dr. King the "I Have a Dream" concept. He was a MAM who was not only brilliant but proud and unashamed; his name was Bayard Rustin. When the conservatives around Dr. King begin to pressure Dr. King about his mentor on his own accord, Rustin walked away from Dr. King, resulting in him being temporally written out of the history of the Civil Rights Movement. When he passed away in 1987, Rustin left a rich legacy that continues to this day.

Bayard Rustin is one of thousands of MAMs who lived their lives out and lived their lives through the power of their authentic authority. He did so during one of the most difficult periods in American history. The rules state, like Rustin, you have the authentic authority to effect change in yourself, in your relationships, within your neighborhood or town, and even where you work.

On Your Authority
GLP Rule 202

What sentence(s) in this rule stands out for you?

How would you define this rule for your social media followers?

On Your Truth
GLP Rule 203

The rules state that when you are living your truth, you have internalized who you are. Once you know who you are, this knowledge allows you to actualize a special warrior spirit deep within. The warrior spirit of confidence projects outwardly in all your accomplishments as well as your learning experiences. One aspect about living your truth is not only understanding who you are but being comfortable with that person from the inside. Over the years, there were several famous MAMs who lived their lives standing in their truth while moving forward.

One of them was a born in 1925 to wealth in Southern California. By the time he was five, both of his parents became alcoholics. To escape the uncertainty in his home, this MAM began to be interested in tap dancing. He enrolled in the same school that other famous stars like Judy Garland and Shirley Temple trained years before. Eventually, his father moved the family to a better part of Los Angles where this MAM began to see movie acting as a way out of his circumstances. It was during that time his extreme good looks were recognized, and while in his late teens, he was cast as a Russian teenager for his first movie role. At the start of World War II, he enlisted in the navy and had his first sexual experience. After he discovered the pleasures of being with another male, it was then he knew who he was supposed to love.

This actor went on to have a long career in productions like *Strangers on a Train* and *Showboat*. However, the movie *Rope* was groundbreaking because of the taboo subject matter about two homosexuals who murdered a man and stuffed the body in a trunk while hosting a penthouse dinner party. The movie was a big hit, and it was directed by the great Alfred Hitchcock. The original play was written in the 1940s when the Hollywood moral code prevented discussion about why two good-looking, affluent men shared an apartment in the middle of Manhattan. It has been written that both he and the other actor played the role as close to edge as possible. He was a big star especially during the 1940s and 1950s. His name was Farley Granger, and he openly loved both men and women, including the great actress Shelly Winters and the famous composer/conductor Leonard Bernstein. During the early 1960s, he met and fell in love with producer Robert Calhoun, and they remained partners for more than forty years.

While Farley Granger died in 2011 at the age of eighty-five, his truth lives on through his movies and television shows, through the theater, and through this quote from his autobiography: *"I was never ashamed, and never felt the need to explain or apologize for my relationships to anyone. I have loved men. I have loved women."*

How will you conduct your life and stand in the truth of who you are as a MAM? The life of Farley Granger is a perfect example of truth and standing for who you are even when the times, the culture, and the circumstances are against you.

He lived during an era where, in some circles, same-sex attraction was called a love that dared not speak its name. The rules state that obstacles men like Farley faced have been somewhat removed for you; how do you take advantage of these opportunities? Farley's truth helped to fuel his place in the upper echelon of acting and as one of the MAM heroes.

What is your passion, your truth? Are you ready to actualize it?

On Your Truth
GLP Rule 203

What sentence(s) in this rule stands out for you?

How would you define this rule for your social media followers?

On Talent
GLP Rule 204

The rules state that there is a talent within you; use it because it is an expression of your internal creation. To have talent means that you possess a natural ability or an aptitude that is above average. There are gifts of genius that exist inside every one of you. These gifts will sustain you as you land on top of your profession or become financially wealthy. There are many MAMs at this moment that are developing the talents that were given to them before birth; why should you be any different? It is never too late to begin actualizing your talent. The rules advise you to take the next steps toward goal direction today. No matter what kind of MAM, you are never buy into the notion that you can't achieve greatness by using your unique talents..

In the 1920s, a young boy was born in New York City in a neighborhood called Harlem. His mother married a preacher, and while her husband was not his natural father, he gave this young boy his last name. He attended the famous DeWitt Clinton High School where he worked on the school paper with another famous MAM named Richard Avedon. Growing up, this teenager knew somehow he was different from the rest of the kids in his neighborhood.

Because of his feminine mannerisms, he was physically abused by his stepfather. This trailblazer wanted community acceptance so badly that as a teenager, he was famous in black American neighborhoods around the East Coast as a child Pentecostal preacher; he had talent. As a young adult, he publicly rejected religion; although in later years, his experience in the Black church influenced most of his great works of Americana. Leaving the Pentecostal Church freed him to express his same-sex attraction and to explore what he became famous for—writing. He moved away from Harlem to live in another part of New York City called the Village. The thinking at that time was that he could live in a neighborhood that accepted him as both a black man and a man who was same-sex attracted.

However, the story goes that after living in the Village for a few years and becoming disillusioned, he decided to join other black artists of that era and left USA to live in Paris, France. Paris allowed him to push beyond what he had been doing as a writer. Living there helped him to take his talents beyond his New York City/USA experience. As an expatriate, he became exposed to a new way of writing. He was one of the first writers who, in nearly all of his publications, included same-sex characters. His friends were Richard Wright, Josephine Baker, Maya Angelou, Nina Simone, Langston Hughes, Medgar Evers, Malcolm X, and Martin Luther King Jr.

He was a prolific talent; his name is James Baldwin, and he is truly one of the great American storytellers.

By the time he returned to the USA in the early 1960s, Baldwin had already written best sellers like *Giovanni's Room, Go Tell It on the Mountain*, and a collection of essays called *Notes of a Native Son*.

Not only did Baldwin use his talents for writing, he was involved in the struggle for civil rights, including protesting the Vietnam War. James Baldwin was a MAM who used his phenomenal talents to grow and to positively affect every area of life he encountered.

During his early years, Baldwin learned how to hone his skills by writing sermons, using a dramatic flair to make the narrative come alive. Then Baldwin used an act of faith to leave the United States and travel far away to discover his muse. His talents allowed him to influence friends and become of part of U.S. history. Baldwin was skillful enough to write more than twenty novels and essays that are read today. He stood with other pioneers in the protest lines and used his talents to fight against war and segregation.

James Baldwin accomplished many goals during his lifetime despite homophobia and racism. Will you do the same in your own way? To use your talent means you are doing what feels good to you and what is good for you. It makes you happy, and it adds value to other's lives. Most importantly, it helps you make money—now that's using your talent! When you allow your talent not to be shown or lie dormant, you are not living a full emotionally healthy life.

On Talent
GLP Rule 204

What sentence(s) in this rule stands out for you?

How would you define this rule for your social media followers?

On Anger
GLP Rule 205

The rules state that one of the most common yet nonproductive emotions you can hold on to is anger. This negative emotion occurs when you defend your integrity, protect your cultural identity, and perceive that your needs have not been met. One aspect of anger occurs when you feel like you have been rejected or someone has made you feel insignificant. The person you are speaking with may not be aware that they have produced these feelings in you, but you feel angry emotions nevertheless. Anger is all about the other person's intent and how you received the message. One response to anger is to automatically defend your legitimacy as a way to protect yourself from rejection. This occurs when you feel social rejection or a rejection of your ideas or alienation of affection from a love one.

Social rejection is how you feel when your name is not on the list of that exclusive club or your close friends were invited to a party, and somehow you were not.

Rejection of your ideas can happen when you work on a project with a group and your name is left off the report or you were denied that promotion. In your life, you are not taken seriously, not because what you have to say isn't important but because the idea comes from you.

Alienation of affection happens, for instance, when a heterosexual friend or family member realizes that you are attracted to the same sex and cut off their relationship with you. A more intimate example of alienation is after years of having a healthy sex life, for some reasons, love making goes from five days a week to five times a year.

Ultimately, when you hear terms like *fag, fairy, nelle, buller, sissy,* and *batty boy,* several feelings are evoked. Each toxic word ignites your defense mechanisms, and this deep reaction forces you to protect your cultural identity. It is quite natural to have an intense reaction when negative words and accusations are targeted toward you or other men who are attracted to the same sex. When you protect your cultural identity, your internal stimuli can react in three different ways: fight, fright, or flight. For example, when you hear the word *faggot,* if you protect your identity with:

Fight; it means that you physically or verbally challenge the person who made the statement;

Fright; it means to either stay silent when you hear that negative word, or your fear forces you to join the person who made the toxic statement;

Flight; it says that you find a way to remove yourself from the person attached to the fag statement; you never allow yourself to be in that person's company.

Fight, fright, or flight: which response best describes you?

Most MAMs will tell you that when around family, at a reunion, or at some other familiar events, even if you are out, somehow your life is not as real as your heterosexual siblings. Just because you may not have a state-sanctioned marriage or you have not fathered children, you are silently told that somehow your life does not matter. Their rationale could be who you love is just a style and therefore irrelevant. When your life is disregarded by family, it can cause you to have negative emotions. Negative emotions, if not recognized or actively worked on, can prevent you from moving forward.

In Great Britain during the 1890s, there was one MAM who allowed his anger to take away his freedom and destroy his successful career; his name was Oscar Wilde. He was famous for such noted literary classics like *The Picture of Dorian Gray* and *The Importance of Being Ernest*; both books had a same-sex attraction subplot.

During Victorian England in the late 1800s, expressing any openly same-sex attraction was forbidden because even the accusation could ruin your reputation. Also, you could be charged with a crime and possibly sent to jail. Several biographers say Wilde used his wife's pregnancy as an excuse to have an affair and to begin to live most of his private life within the homosexual London underground. He was introduced to a younger spoiled MAM named Lord Alfred. Lord Alfred's father was a marquess, a royal position of patronage. It was the marquess who confronted Wilde about his secret life. He called Wilde a sodomite and warned him to stay away from his son.

Wilde, against the advice of his friends, allowed his anger to guide him. He attempted to publicly sue the marquess for libel. He did this while in the middle of enjoying the success for the play, *The Importance of Being Ernest*; the marquees countersued Wilde. He charged Oscar Wilde with committing homosexual acts. There was a public trial; both Wilde and his family were humiliated. Wilde allowed negative emotions to control his rational thinking; he didn't consider that his down low MAM friends were not happy with the public spotlight, so even they helped the English court find Wilde guilty of sodomy. Oscar Wilde was sent to prison where he served two years of hard labor. He was really never the same after that experience and died in France at the age of forty-six, penniless. It wasn't until many years after his death that Oscar Wilde's artistic reputation was restored.

What happened was that Wilde decided to ignore his close friends' advice and allowed the marquess to control his emotions. He was caught up in an anger cycle, which clouded his judgment. It was this cycle that created the unfortunate circumstances before, during, and after Wilde's infamous trial. The rules remind you that anger is a natural state, but it can be controlled so that its effects are temporary and do not become a part of who you are as a human being.

When have you allowed your own anger to guide your reactions?

How do you know when anger has taken over your rational judgment?

What have you lost as a result of your actions?

What lessons did you learn about this emotion and your response?

On Anger
GLP Rule 205

What sentence(s) in this rule stands out for you?

How would you define this rule for your social media followers?

On Coming Out
GLP Rule 206

The rule on coming out or revealing your MAM nature is that it's not a one-time process. Coming out is an action that will have to be repeated depending on the persons, places, and things you interact with throughout you life experience. Even if you have not publicly made an announcement about your same-sex attraction, you come out every time you meet someone you are attracted to. It is a fact that each time you intimately connect with another individual or when you are among your circle of friends/family, you come out. There are those of you who may have only come out to mom or a sibling or an aunt, or an uncle. In other words, you limit the family members to a few but not discussed it with the rest. Those examples mimic the ways men who are attracted to the same sex to naturally reveal themselves to other close individuals in their lives as well. You had the coming-out discussion because instinctively you knew that one of them understood you.

When thinking about publicly declaring who you are, many of you consider the Bible, homophobia, and even violence. How much value do you place on these external pressures when making the coming out decision? Whomever you come out to, the bottom line is another person has knowledge about you; standing strong about who you are is important after that revelation. Going public is extremely stressful and anxiety producing for many MAMs because not every heterosexual has the same level of comfortably.

Coming out to others is measured carefully by each individual who's experiencing it. You ask questions like what does coming out mean to me, and who will be the first to know?

How will revealing who I am affect my personal and financial security?

Do I have a talent that stands above the rest, or am I guided by my secrets? Once you've answered these questions, you will know if the timing is right for coming out publicly. The point is, no one can tell you how or when to come out, but when you do, life can be liberating.

MAMs have been coming out in their own ways for years. For example, way back in the 1930s, 1940s, and 1950s, there was one famous pioneering movie director. He was able to come out with most of his famous friends, even though the public had no idea about his sexuality.

His movies included pictures like *The Philadelphia Story*, *The Women*, *My Fair Lady*, and he even directed the beginning of *Gone with the Wind*. During his prime, he became the unofficial host of the MAM Hollywood "on the low" culture. It has been documented that each Sunday afternoon he would host same-sex gatherings that included people like Noel Coward, Cole Porter, Somerset Maugham, William Haines, Alan Ladd, and many other golden age industry creative elites. The party favors were many young attractive MAMs whom they met in parks, bars, and gyms. This movie director was even arrested for what was called back then vice charges. The studio he worked for at that time kept the arrest from the papers and had the court records expunged. This Academy Award and Golden Globe winning movie director was George Cukor, and he lived his life, at least in Hollywood and New York, as an out MAM but only to his circle of close friends. The bottom line is that the decision to come out always reveals itself individually.

On Coming Out
GLP Rule 206

What sentence(s) in this rule stands out for you?

How would you define this rule for your social media followers?

On Being Defined By Who You Sleep With
GLP Rule 207

Never allow anyone to judge you because of whom you are attracted to or whom you have in your bed. A large number of heterosexuals believe that all MAMs are attracted to anyone who is male. Many of them cannot understand that outside of work or school environments, if you are seen talking to another male, then the two of you must be having sexual relations. There is a bias revealed when you hear these assumptions. News flash, as a MAM, you have an internal compass or filter that allows you to know when your type comes along.

It is true that you have a type, but it is not true that you already know what that type is or what that type looks like. Who you feel attracted to is guided by an internal mechanism so deep inside of you; it's subconscious, and chances are you are not aware of it. There are times, as a man who is attracted to the same sex, you will find yourself attracted to someone who may have had a different growing-up experience than you had. Even your circle of friends may attempt to judge you because for instance, as an attorney, you are in a relationship with someone who has had a criminal background. Here's a rule for professionals: as long as you are not crossing any ethical boundaries or breaking state, federal, or moral laws, who is in your bed should not affect your professional profile.

Several years ago, during the twentieth century, there was a famous MAM journalist who would not allow others to define him because of who shared his bed. He was born in 1910, to a very old Connecticut family, and he was the nephew of Pres. Theodore Roosevelt and a cousin to Pres. Franklyn Roosevelt. His name was Joseph Alsop, and he was a Harvard-educated journalist who remained at the top of his profession for more than forty years. He was a noted foreign correspondent; he wrote for many New York papers of the day. He published a syndicated newspaper piece that was the first of its kind. Although he was a Republican, he had ties to Democratic administrations as well. He was married briefly late in life, but it was an open secret in his lifetime that Alsop was a practicing MAM.

During the communist scare of the 1950s, he was accused of being what Senator McCarthy called a pervert, a judgment made by McCarthy because of who Alsop slept with. The Soviet Union's KGB photographed Alsop having sex with another man and blackmailed him for twenty years.

J. Edgar Hoover, the FBI chief, who was also attracted to the same sex kept a file on Alsop. Hoover eventually leaked it around Washington. One of his lovers, an appointment secretary to Pres. Dwight Eisenhower, had to resign his post because of the contents contained in the FBI file. Even in the 1970s, when Alsop was headed for retirement, the KGB sent the old sex photos to other journalists anyway.

However, despite the Soviet Union, McCarthyism, and the FBI preconceived notions, Alsop refused to be defined by sexuality or false accusations. By confronting these issues, not only did Joseph Alsop defend his rights, but it can also be surmised that throughout his life, he refused to be defined by who slept in his bed. What about you? Insert your story here!

On Being Defined By Who You Sleep With
GLP Rule 207

What sentence(s) in this rule stands out for you?

How would you define this rule for your social media followers?

On Greatness
GLP Rule 208

The rules state that there is a universal path which will lead you to greatness, and this is achieved after you find peace in the life you have chosen for yourself. There will be a few challenges or roadblocks getting there, but it will turn out all right, and your dreams will be actualized. This happens because there is a unique spirit in all MAMs that allows you to sore as high as you can go in life. If you are going to fly as high as you can, each MAM must start believing that self-actualization or greatness can be achieved in the first place.

How do you know that you are on the path to greatness? The answer is that it's looks differently for each individual. However, there are commonalities that exist for all who achieve greatness in their lives. Some commonalities include having the dream since childhood. More listening and less talking are traits; trust in your internal belief compass. Exceeding your grasp by going above average is important. Capitalizing on your accomplishments and learning from your mistakes is key. Frankly, being a role model and fighting for the rights of others are all qualities of greatness.

Several years ago, a movie called *The English Patient* was a popular film. While the movie's protagonist was heterosexual, the truth is the film is based on the life of Laszlo Almasy. In real life, he was a man who is attracted to the same sex. He was born in today's Austria more than a century ago. Almasy's parents were wealthy, and they sent him to England to further his education. He joined World War I, and it has been reported that he became "close" to the king of Austria who bestowed on Almasy the title of count.

It has been documented that he was a famous race car driver and a world-class hunter. In the late twenties and early thirties, Almasy was also an explorer who mapped many places in northern and central Africa not known to the Western world at that time. During World War II, he was accused of being a double agent by both the British and the Italians. Almasy became the ultimate spy. Once, he posed as a German officer and helped the Italians arrest several German agents. When World War II ended, he was arrested by the Soviet Union, but the British helped him escape imprisonment.

Achieving all these acts of greatness did not prevent Almasy from enjoying same-sex intimacy from the average secret service enlistee to royalty. He continued to live a life of achievement until his death in 1951. He became a great MAM because Laszlo Almasy was able to understand what attributes he had, and he used those qualities to master every endeavor in which he participated.

If Almasy's life was not great enough for you, then consider this tea: The great emancipator, the president who held the nation together and freed the slaves shared his bed with three men during his lifetime. As young man, he met and lived with Billy Green; their bed was so small that today's twin-size bed would be big compared to it. The years right before marriage, Abraham Lincoln lived with Joshua Speed. Speed was a fine, good-looking man; it is documented that they lived together for about four years.

The story goes when Speed left him to return to his family's plantation to marry; Lincoln was so traumatize by Speed's departure that he went into a clinical depression and was on a suicide watch for a few months.

During the civil war, Lincoln was so involved in the battles that for a time, he left his family to actually be at the war front. While there, he met and slept with an officer by the name of David Derickson. They were often seen in the White House together after hours. Moreover, they were seen going to plays and other public events, without Mary. It is said that Lincoln never lost contact with these men whom he shared a bed.

What do you think? Was our sixteenth president a male who is attracted to the same sex? Did he allow himself to be defined by who he slept with?

Did he allow his close male relationships to affect his greatness?

Do the research. Remember, facts matter and let others share the answers to these questions with you. If it is true about President Lincoln, then each of you has something to aspire toward—the sky is your only limit!

On Greatness
GLP Rule 208

What sentence(s) in this rule stands out for you?

How would you define this rule for your social media followers?

How to Get What You Deserve
GLP Rule 209

The rules tell you that as a MAM, you should always strive to improve your emotional and intellectual well-being; it's how you get what you deserve. This goal can be accomplished by giving yourself permission to take advantage of every opportunity that offers advancement. Allowing circumstances, for example, to block your graduation, certification, or licenses is unacceptable. Take on the challenges offered to you by your employers, it will pay off later. Try to get noticed by using the systems where you work to your advantage. Pay close attention to work-related politics and understand your worth. Ask for that raise; if the answer is affirmative or negative, your confidence is strengthened because you asked. Promotion or no promotion, raise or no raise, strive to better you. Study, practice, and learn all you can to move forward in your career. Timing is everything. Remember, there is always more for you to learn. Alexander Pope said it best: *"A little learning is a dangerous thing. Drink deep, taste not the Pierian Spring. There shallow draughts intoxicate the brain and drinking largely sobers us again . . ."*

One MAM who used those principles to get what he deserved was born in Los Angles in the late 1940s; his name was Sylvester James. As a child, he studied every female gospel singer of the day.

Having been encouraged by his grandmother, Sylvester first became famous throughout Southern California as a child gospel singer. As a teenager, he began to understand his attractions and how to be comfortable in his own skin. While on his sexuality journey, the onset of adolescence caused, shall we say, drama between Sylvester, his mother, and stepfather. Despite these conflicts, Sylvester completed high school and attended beauty school. It was around this time that he used what he learned there to transform himself into an artist that was not only musically talented, but he introduced the androgynous persona to the public.

Known as the drag queen of dance music, Sylvester started his career when he moved to San Francisco in the late 1960s. It was at that time he joined the locally famous drag group called the Cockettes. Shortly after leaving the group, Sylvester knew he had the ability to get what he deserved. Before his life ended at the age of forty-one, he had three no. 1 records on the Billboard charts: "You Make Me Feel (Mighty Real)",

"Dance (Disco Heat)", and "Someone Like You." Also, the disco fueled double entendre; "Do You Wanna Funk" is a dance classic. He launched the careers of Martha Wash and Izora Rhodes; he worked with the Pointer Sisters, Patti Labelle, and he provided backup vocals for Aretha Franklin. Sylvester had fourteen studio albums and forty-one singles; his famous live album, the only one he made in his career, gave the world a rendition of a Patti Labelle's song called "You Are My Friend." As member of The Dance Music Hall of Fame, Sylvester has inspired many other artists who have come after him. The rules ask you: How will you get what you deserve? What will be your legacy?

How to Get What You Deserve
GLP Rule 209

What sentence(s) in this rule stands out for you?

How would you define this rule for your social media followers?

You and Your Circle of Friends
GLP Rule 210

The rules state that the key to your emotional healing is understanding the influence of your cultural identification. Culture in this instance has to do with your family, where you are from, the role religion plays in your life, and where you plan to go in the future. A roadblock to learning how to heal eternalized shame and validate yourself is to cherish one of the most important resources in this life—your circle of family/friends or CFFs. The CFFs may not be related to you by blood, but they are related to you by love. It is a general rule that no matter what community you reside in across the United States or in another country, as a MAM, you should have a tight group of CFFs. They are the ones who are there with you no matter what you may go through. Your CFFs provide you with emotional sustenance. They are your lifeline. You share secrets, you hang out together, and you even establish your own unwritten rules with each other. Did you notice the concept of CFF purposely does not have the word *forever* in its definition?

As the years go by, it's okay to think about taking an objective view of your CFFs and replace them as needed. If you take no actions to critically review your circle of family/friends, then you may be held back.

According to the rules, there are times when some of your friendships, no matter how close you are to them, can grow apart or even look different. Some may ask how do I know when someone in my CFF is moving away from me? What does this change mean to me as a person?

If you have the ability to internally heal and validate your own spirit on a frequent basis, then having others around for that purpose is not that important. No one else can do that for you. The only path to self-healing is for you to find out what in your life has blocked your forward motion.

Forward motion can be blocked because you may not have addressed what occurred in your life before the onset of adolescence. The age before adolescences is important to review; most mental health professionals will tell you by the time you're twelve years old your core personality and values have already been developed.

Adolescence is another period in your life that can be examined as you review what could be blocking your healing. Keep in mind while there is a core personality already developed, any disruption or trauma during this time can result in long-lasting emotional scars that continue well into adulthood. These scars are identified by psychiatrist, psychologist, and licensed social workers/therapists as personality disorders. Currently, there are around ten identified personality disorders. Mental health evidence says these many of these disorders are a result of a traumatic childhood experience. Personality disorders are different from personality traits.

A personality trait can be explained as ways you perceive, think about, and relate to the world. For example, you can change your hair, clothes, etc., but you will be the same inside; you'll just look different. If you have a personality disorder, you tend to relate to the world in the same way, in all situations. If you are mentally healthy person, you use different aspects of your personality that are appropriate to the situation. For example, you don't act the same way in the office as you do with your circle of family/friends. But the person who has a personality disorder can only relate to these situations one way.

Personality disorder can occur in an individual who has had experience with extreme emotional, physical, or sexual abuse in their lives as children. Not surprisingly, the primary problem is difficulty maintaining ongoing relationships. For example, that friend may be very charming, friendly, and likeable when you first meet him. Once this individual with personality disorder gets close to you, he will begin to feel frightened and resentful about how much he needs you. This often results in the individual attacking or rejecting you because you are unable to meet his needs. As a matter of fact, it is impossible to meet his needs no matter how hard you try. If he has personality disorder, his worldview is black or white with no grey area. This individual is either all supportive of you, or he is rejecting you at every turn. There is no middle ground for him. Within your CFFs, the one with a personality disorder will often try to turn you against each other.

If you have someone in your circle of friends with a personality disorder, then you must do several things to protect your own emotional health. Don't take what he says personally; people with this issue will have many demands and never feel satisfied. It's important that everyone in your circle of friends give him the same message. It is okay to listen to him, but don't get too involved. If you recognize that he is creating issues with others friends, don't take sides. Realize that it's okay to be angry at times. Remember, the individual is not doing this on purpose; he is really unaware that he functions this way. Therapy and, in some small cases, a medication evaluation is recommended for friends with these issues.

CFFs are a necessary positive aspect of same sex life. In spite of these human obstacles, it will serve you well to cherish, maintain, and accept the evolution of yours as the years go by.

You and Your Circle of Friends
GLP Rule 210

What sentence(s) in this rule stands out for you?

How would you define this rule for your social media followers?

The Rules on Style, Intimacy, and Making a Connection

The SIMC Rules 400–410

The rules for style, intimacy, and making a connection, also known as the SIMC rules, cover a wide range of need to know information of culture for males who are attracted to the same sex. These sets of rules provoke thought and stimulate conversation about what's important in the world you inhabit as males who are attracted to the same sex. With that goal in mind, the rules in this chapter start with the importance of appearance—how you appear to yourself and how you appear to others. Caring about how you look and your physical attributes is something that you share with all MAMs. When you think about it, the first thing you notice about someone else is their physical appearance. The importance of your own style, swagger, especially your physique, is key to how other men perceive you. Whether your style is conservative, casual, trendy, or alternative, it belongs to you, and you are required to work it, for all its worth! Style demands that you are able to look at your reflection and say, *I'm worthy. I matter, and there is not a man alive more handsome than me.* If you are transvestite or a drag queen, your refection will inspire you to say, *I'm worthy. I matter, and there is not a queen currently reigning more beautiful than me.*

When you meet another man, in many cases, his face and his body type is your first attraction. He has to be physically appealing; it's important to note that what may appeal to you may not appeal to others; it's an individual choice. Always feel confident in what turns you on; let no one sway your resolve. In addition to the face and the body, an intimate connection between two males cannot happen unless there is a vibe.

A *vibe* is another word for that familiar energy each man feels when they are introduced to others in a social setting. Another rule in this chapter helps you understand that it's not just what you have but how you are living with what you have that matters. How others see you is important, and how you maintain your environment speaks volumes to the larger society. There are some distinct characteristics, mannerisms, and vernacular that link all MAMs, no matter where you come from. Words, its terminology and definitions take on a different meaning when spoken by you. Included are rules written in this chapter to explain the language differential. After all, language is one identifier used to distinguish cultures. Therefore, because of language, it's worth repeating that men who are attracted to the same have their own culture within the larger society.

Marriage or intimate relationships, what they look like, and how to build a foundation with another male are addressed. Included in this chapter are rules concerning different kinds of MAMs, like bisexuals, transvestites, and drag queens. Cursing is explained from online activity to meeting him in person.

There are also rules concerning how to recognize when other men who are attracted to the same sex are in the room with you, but their sexual preference is not obvious. Some MAMs, as with the larger population, may find it difficult to cope with the pressures of adulthood and act out by experimenting with substances and other addictions. Several rules cover this aspect of life.

Addictive behaviors can have a negative impact on moving forward with your life goals. Therefore, the rules help you avoid those traps so that you can live your life in style, make good connections, and have healthy intimate relationships. Let's read on!

On Style, Beating Your Mug, and Affectation
SIMC Rule 401

If you are a man who is attracted to the same sex, then you have a conscious sense of your own unique style, swagger, and MAM elegance. Style is reminding others you have entered the room just by your physical presence. It is an understanding that your sense of elegance or swagger sets you apart from everyone else. Style, swagger, and elegance for you is not just about what appears on the outside, but it's the confidence in which you navigate your life overall. Staying healthy is an important aspect of this rule; you are what you eat, and exercise cannot be ignored. While style is not just about what you wear, fashion does play a critical role. Take notice. Remember, dress to impress yourself first. Afterward, you're ready to step out in public having a unique attitude you have arrived.

> ... Attitude is an intrinsic part of how an ensemble comes together. Climate, occasion, culture, cost . . . attitude comes from within and is translated in your daily choice of threads (Lloyd Boston, *Men of Color: Fashion, History, Fundamentals*, 1998).

There is a real cultural desire to stay on the cutting edge of fashion, but at the same time, you know how to exhibit your own flare. As a MAM, your style is not totally dictated by trends, but it's rooted in your same-sex ability to make your look appropriate for the occasion. The pants, the shirts, the suits, the hats, the accessories, and what you have on your feet are all you need to begin to build your style reputation. No matter what age you are today, if you keep in mind that you are classic, you are hot, you are happening, then you can't go wrong.

On Style, Beating Your Mug, and Affectation
SIMC Rule 401

What sentence(s) in this rule stands out for you?

How would you define this rule for your social media followers?

On Beating Your Mug
SIMC 401 B

The rules states that playing a big role in your style is how you take care of your mug. The mug is just another name for your face. At times, you will hear someone says "beating my mug." *Beating your mug* is a term used to express the importance of how you take care of your face. How you wash it, scrub it, or paint it displays your pride and health. No matter your skin texture, cleansing your face is a daily necessity. Removing facial hair is important; some men can shave daily, for others, waiting a few days in between are just as effective. If you choose to have facial hair, then trimming it is a must. Other hygiene rules to investigate are using sponges that are recommended to exfoliate your skin during bathing. Some agree that using washcloths on a regular basis is prohibited, although you may use them when you have guests.

A portion of the MAM community expresses themselves by living all or a part of their lives as trannys or drag queens. For this part of the community, beating your mug is sport. Painting your face requires foundation or base that is close to your skin tone. Liquid is the best because it will blend better. The eyebrow pencil, lashes, rouge, and lipstick are all the basic ingredients. The key to making sure your mug is flawless is lighting; make sure when applying paint and powder, you, some agree, do so under as much light as possible. Always start with the contours of your facial structure. Once you have done so, very few will be able to, as they say, *"spook your carrying ons."*

On Beating Your Mug
SIMC Rule 401B

What sentence(s) in this rule stands out for you?

How would you define this rule for your social media followers?

On Affectation
SIMC Rule 401C

Make sure your hair is neat, whether it's long or short; there has to be a style in the haircut or the coiffure. The feet should be clean, free of long toenails, and ready to be viewed on a hot summer day or appreciated during a sexual moment. If you do nothing else, clean or trim your fingernails. Unless you are a drag queen or tranny, some say polish is passé for men; having your nails buffed is better, but it's all up to you. Before leaving your home for the day or to attend that event, make sure you give yourself one last look in the mirror. Here, lighting is key as well. Full lighting in your home near the mirrors acts just like the sunlight outside; check yourself and make adjustments accordingly. When you step out the door door no matter what happened in your home or how you feel in the moment; you are in the public eye. It's show time! In addition, when using scents, like cologne or oil, make sure you use just enough to stand out but not so much it overpowers everyone else. When choosing cologne, make sure it mixes well with your own body scent as well. Stick with a scent that can become your trademark and update it accordingly. The same rule applies to jewelry and other embellishments; less is always more.

When out with friends or family members, if you smoke cigarettes, stop! But if you can't right now, please make sure you carry chewing gum or mints and a tube of some sort of scented lotion with you at all times. Wash your hands and use the lotion after the cigarette; the scent of stale smoke could be a turn off for dates and others you intimately interact with. By the way, washing hands regularly is just the healthy thing for a man to do, especially after using the bathroom.

On Affectation
SIMC Rule401C

What sentence(s) in this rule stands out for you?

How would you define this rule for your social media followers?

In Your Villa and Holding Court
SIMC 402

Home should be a special place that represents who you really are. Some of you may live in a room or an apartment, or you may even own a big house or a mansion. Calling a place home or your villa is a serious declaration; it is a reflection of your personality, representing the natural side of you. The home you live in should always be comfortable and inviting. It is your duty to ensure there is a sense of tranquility in your space. Negative energy should be quickly removed; you have a right not to have conflict where you dwell. By doing so, others who are fortunate enough to be invited to your space feel at peace and relaxed. Consider plants and/or flowers in your space. Some say it makes a home cheerful. Having a pet, like a dog or cat, speaks volumes about you in a positive way. Cleaning up behind your pet is essential; for as much as possible, make sure your home is odor and lent free.

Guests invited for that special gathering in your home is a testament to the fact that you have arrived. It says you are the center of gravity with your peer group, and you know how to hold court. When guest arrive in your home they should see a clean orderly space. There should be items in your home that are conversation pieces, like pictures, posters, or tastily arranged artifacts. The rule here is that when someone comes to your home for the first time, a positive impression is created. As the host, make sure you are welcoming and have something interesting to say to each of your guests, especially if the person came with someone else. It is assumed that he will not know any of the guests.

When hosting a small gathering, be sure to encourage conversations between those who may not be familiar with each other. If you know the guests in your home, as the host, you should know at least two guests who will have something in common for general conversation. A good host knows how to make all who enters the home feel included. While you should never run out of food and drink, this rule does not mean you have to financially sponsor the whole gathering either; but if you can, you should.

As a guest, when invited to someone's home, it goes against the rules to intrude on your host privacy without permission. These things include touching items without permission, asking your host to change their music or television channel. A good host knows what atmosphere to create when company arrives. Never make suggestions unless told to do so. Snooping is prohibited; this rule applies to closed doors, medicine cabinets, and other private areas in your host's home. Also know when to leave the party. If the host says it's getting late, catch the hint and then go. If you remain there after your host's request, then you are violating his space. Besides, the energy you spend staying where you are not wanted is not worth the rewards of moving on. First-time guest should always bring a small gift like a bottle of wine, flowers, or something that shows an acknowledgment of thanks for being invited. If you are a frequent guest, as a gesture of appreciation, you should contribute to the food or beverage with either money or in-kind donations. One more rule to consider: if you have not been invited, then it is ill advised for you to show up at someone's door as a surprise. Keep in mind: today, there are many forms of communication. Showing up to his home without permission does not make good sense.

In Your Villa and Holding Court
SIMC 402

What sentence(s) in this rule stands out for you?

How would you define this rule for your social media followers?

On Reading, Shade, Trade, and on the Low
SIMC Rule 403

Cultural terminology or slang has been used by most world-societies, especially since the twentieth century. Slang terminology, according to the rules, is defined as the art of phrasing words in a way that may not be appropriate or accepted when conducting business or when in educated settings. There are many Americans, especially people of color, who have to live their lives in both worlds. For instance, you speak in your cultural vernacular within the community, and you use more standard English when in mainstream society. Unlike other cultural groups, terminology or slang of people who attracted to the same sex contains a rich mixture of wit, irony, and insightful observations. As a MAM, no matter who you are or where you are from, when you hear this kind of terminology used, then you know like-minded men are around. While there are hundreds of slang words used by MAMs, the terms *reading, shade, trade,* and *on the low* are understood by almost all when spoken within the community of people who are attracted to the same sex. There are even MAMs who have created their own language called Argul, a form of pig-latin.

On Reading, Shade, Trade, and on the Low
SIMC Rule 403

What sentence(s) in this rule stands out for you?

How would you define this rule for your social media followers?

Reading
SIMC Rule 403B

The library is opened; now don't come for me unless I send for you queen! There comes a time in every MAM's life when you are called upon to read someone. To read means to use verbal observations as a weapon to degenerate another with your worldview of the facts. Reading can be used as an offensive or as a defensive strategy. The rules state that it is perfectly okay to read someone if you are doing so to protect yourself against emotional harm. As an emotionally healthy MAM, you should never read to inflict pain or suffering on the other person without good cause. On the other hand, real life gets in the way compelling you to let someone have it by slinging an expert read!

Here's how to do it: an expert can analyze you quickly, find your flaws, and read you for points from there. In order to truly learn the art of reading, you have to train yourself to observe and listen. The training materials you'll need are the great dramatic novels and classic movies with strong female leads, as listed in rule no. 410. When reading, timing and delivery are very important. Never read when you are uncomfortable in the environment or intimidated by the other person. The bottom line is in the same-sex community, reading is truly fundamental. Now go among the masses and read my children; read because it had to be done, read for filth, read for those who can't do it for themselves!

Reading
SIMC 403B

What sentence(s) in this rule stands out for you?

How would you define this rule for your social media followers?

Shade
SIMC Rule 403C

The term *shade* describes behavioral affectations that use the double entendre to draw attention to yourself either in a positive or negative manner. It's sarcasm in its highest form; shade is subtle, but its effects are felt by the person on the receiving end. Unlike reading, shade has more to do with body language and affectation, but shade can happen verbally as well. Shade is all about how your actions provoke emotions in others. When you hear the term *throwing shade* or *being shady*, this refers mostly to what you're not saying to individuals who caused you harm. In addition, shade is about using your body language as a defense mechanism because you feel somehow threatened. Shade is very subtle; you know it when you experience it, and everyone else in the room recognizes shade when it happens. Shadiness is about having mystery in the delivery of your bullet. In other words, it's the element of surprise; they don't see it coming.

    A few examples of shade include saying you don't recognize someone when you really do. You're in a meeting; you cause a subtle attention to yourself just to distract the speaker with whom you disagree. When you know that your friend likes the guy across the room, yet you take the guy for yourself. Even how you work an outfit can be shady, like purposely being overly dressed for a social event. Shade is a time-honored MAM tradition passed down from generation to generation in the community.

Shade
SIMC Rule 403C

What sentence(s) in this rule stands out for you?

How would you define this rule for your social media followers?

Trade
SIMC Rule 403D

According to *Webster's Dictionary*, the word *trade* is a noun defined as *the business of buying or selling or bartering commodities*. In the world of MAMs, the term *trade* can be used as both a noun and as an adjective. Trade used as an adjective describes a male penis display. For example, you may hear someone make a statement like, *he's got trade down to his knees*, or *did you see his trade in those pants*? This is a reference to his sexual organ.

As a noun, it is a name usually given to a bisexual or a down-low MAM who is so closeted that he does not commit to interpersonal relationships with other men who are attracted to the same sex. An example: *I heard that he's your piece of trade, or oh, you know, Bo, everyone at the club says he's trade, no matter how many women he dates!*

As you can tell, one word can generate different meanings in the community of men who are attracted to the same sex. Here's to you and your trade, and here's hoping that your trade is enough for him tonight.

Trade
SIMC Rule 403D

What sentence(s) in this rule stands out for you?

How would you define this rule for your social media followers?

On the Low
SIMC Rule 403E

DL or down low has been widely misrepresented by the media and by some authors. According to the rules, DL describes a MAM who is mostly closeted and uncomfortable with the notion of declaring his sexuality in a public way. If a man is on the DL, then it means he is attracted to the same, but his relationships are a secret, not revealed to family and friends. Many DL men are attracted to like-minded individuals, especially when out in public. If you are on the low, then for as much as possible, you try to avoid MAMs who outwardly display stereotypical behavior. Also, there are many DLs who participate in MAM events or go to gay bars and clubs but are not out to neighbors or coworkers. If you are one of these men, then being attached to a label because you are attracted to the same sex is problematic. More importantly, for the person who is DL, there is a psychological fear of being publicly identified as a man who is attracted to the same sex.

It's unfortunate that while as a DL, you go through great lengths to keep your secret; in most cases, others may already have assumptions about your sexuality. There many reasons for these assumptions; some could include your own mannerisms, your attire, your conversations, including what you are not saying when the subject of the opposite sex comes up.

When in the company of other MAMs, your boundaries should be respected. If you are DL, the decision to come out or not is yours alone to make.

On the Low
SIMC Rule 403 E

What sentence(s) in this rule stands out for you?

How would you define this rule for your social media followers?

On Substance Use and Sexual Addiction
SIMC Rule 404

Mind-altering substances and other pharmaceuticals are popular with some in the MAM community. Substance use affects all segments of society. This rule primarily applies to possible addictions common among a segment of men who are attracted to the same sex. The rule is if mind-altering substances are used more than a few times, you could become psychologically and physically dependent. In the community, cigarettes, alcohol, and marijuana are known as the foundation drugs. With the exception of marijuana, addiction to these drugs can hurt you physically. Cigarettes have a deadly reputation for a reason. Alcohol is a particularly nasty addiction because it's socially acceptable; by the time you want help, there's damage to your liver, and there are other health concerns. Moderation with these substances is just the smart thing to do. Socialize, go through your phase, but know when it ends.

In the United States, the history of addiction and substance use as an epidemic began in the later part of the nineteenth century. The first drug the nation became hooked on was cocaine. In the late 1800s, the population expanded west, and so did the cure-all medicines. These medicines were sold by peddlers who, in many cases, misrepresented themselves as doctors. Today, these peddlers, notions men, or Dr. Feelgoods are portrayed in movies about the old west. The cure-all medications they sold contained large amounts of cocaine along with morphine.

Back then, these substances were in items like toothpaste, cough syrups, headache powders, and even a popular drink called Coca-Cola. By 1914, the USA created drug prohibition laws to primarily address the widespread addiction that occurred during the early twentieth century. These laws have existed from that time and continue today. Crack cocaine created an epidemic in many parts of the USA during the 1980s and 1990s. Even now, some supernovas and ikonoclass struggle to recover from crack addiction.

Moreover, methamphetamine has been affecting the MAM community since the beginning of the twenty-first century. Mind-altering substances like crystal meth, Tina, G, XTC, e-pills, mollies, and roofies are classified as stimulants because they affect the central nervous system. Particularly G, roofies, special K, e-pills, and XTC are used in same-sex club events and the circuit parties; these drugs are mostly tasteless and odorless. When these substances are combined with alcohol, they can distort perceptions of sight and sound. In addition, they leave you with memory loss and a detachment from reality. Rohypnol and GHB are also called the date-rape drugs. Does it mean you can't attend a circuit party because you are not using these substances? Some argue that the good thing is circuit parties are great way to enjoy same sex fun, if done with maybe a little alcohol, weed, coffee, or another caffeine beverage.

The effect of crystal meth or Tina—its street name paying homage to the great singing icon Tina Turner—literally feels like when Tina "turns it" on stage. This substance is on the rise with many in the ingénue and supernova stages of same-sex development.

Crystal meth is one of the few substances that can be snorted, smoked, or injected. Some addicts even reused this substance through their urine as well! First established as a weight loss drug, meth's euphoric feelings can last for more than eight hours. However, it's the side effects that are attractive to its users. For some, this substance causes an increase in your sexual libido. On many dating/hookup apps, Tina is used in what's called the party-n-play community (PNP), often consisting of meth threesomes and meth orgies. Addiction to this drug happens so rapidly that even receiving a kiss from someone who just inhaled it can make you feel euphoric, so beware of the "crystal kiss."

When you become addicted to substances, it means you are unable to stop your self-destructive behavior. When this occurs, your relationship is breaking up, you are in financial disaster, you have lost your job, and you have engaged in activities to risk your life. Addiction is a compulsive behavior that completely dominates the addict's life. You make the high a priority, more important than anything else. Addicts are willing to sacrifice anything in the pursuit of reaching that initial high, which is never achieved after the first time. Addiction ages your face faster than time ever could. It causes depression resulting in you not finding freedom until you are fortunate enough to realize that you are sick and tired of being sick and tired!

In order to truly remain substance free, you must passionately want it. There's no one else in your life who can want to be drug free more than you. Always remember since 1935, recovery has been proven to be a real thing, so keep coming back! It's up to you to make your own choices about substance use, including alcohol and cigarettes.

On Substance Use and Sexual Addiction
SIMC Rule 404

What sentence(s) in this rule stands out for you?

How would you define this rule for your social media followers?

Sexual Addiction
SIMC Rule 404B

According to published studies, sexual addiction is a real behavioral disease. This behavior affects a small percentage of the overall population. Research states in the same-sex community, the addiction numbers can double. Although the number is low, the issue is significant enough for the rules to bring it to your attention.

If you are a sex addict, then the same pattern that defined substance use reveals itself in sexual addiction. Sex addiction makes the act of having sex a priority, more important than any other part of life. If you are a sex addict, you focused on the conquest. Often, you tend to ignore rational thinking, embracing anxiety-laden situations instead. As an addict, your awareness is impaired, and self-protection is ignored. This risky behavior can cause you to contract sexually transmitted diseases, including HIV/AIDS. This addiction can even cause you to become a victim of crime which could end with violent consequences.

When you have this diagnosis, sexual acts, pornography, pay-to-play situations, and sex parties all provide you with a sensual high. The point is, as an addict, you become dependent on external sexual stimuli to feel whole. The addict substitutes healthy relationships for unhealthy ones. Many addicts are hypersexual, seeking sexual intercourse or ejaculation many times during a twenty-four-hour period.

Some addicted MAMs seek out multiple affairs because of the euphoria that comes from the thrill of the chase. This particular behavior is about the conquest rather than the sexual experience itself. This is true especially for those addicts who are in positions of authority.

Many sex addicts have mostly these three things in common; they were either emotionally, sexually, or physically abused before late adolescence.

There is help for the MAM who have been identified as a sex addict; you can recover. Treatment includes support groups, along with individual psychotherapy to get on a healthy track. If your addiction is linked with mental illness or chemical imbalance in the brain, usually, anti-depressants prescribed and monitored by a psychiatrist is an appropriate evaluation. Sex addiction is a serious phenomenon within the community. Keep in mind: there are many MAMs like you who have a healthy appetite for sex; this does not mean you have an addiction or you engage in risky behavior.

Sexual Addiction
SIMC Rule 404B

What sentence(s) in this rule stands out for you?

How would you define this rule for your social media followers?

On Being Crafty
SIMC Rule 405

There will always be a small percentage of men who are attracted to the same sex that will engage in the dark arts of craft or stunt pulling. Being crafty or pulling a stunt simply means engaging in mischievous or illegal behaviors which can lead to criminal prosecution. The characteristics of MAMs that participates in this kind of activity are usually either addicted to substances or may have a sexual addiction. Then there are some who may simply enjoy the adrenaline rush of breaking the law. The MAM who is crafty knows how to lift bank code numbers off of checking accounts or credit cards and cash them in under his name. He can send you a computer virus and invade your privacy.

Prescription fraud is another simple task easily accomplished with this type of behavior. Clothing stores with all their camera security and alarm codes cannot stop him from stealing or boosting whatever outfits you need. The really good ones are able to abscond with items in your exact size!

As a buyer, you say to yourself, "There's' nothing like something falling off a truck and landing in your wardrobe." The point here is when you receive these ill-gotten goods, you are providing the crafty one with a customer base.

In addition, when you cheat on your taxes, sublease your rental apartment, received double payments and not report it, you are being crafty as well. These types of crimes are considered white collar or nonviolent; they are in most cases committed for financial gain. The only way to really have financial security is to perform honest work that provides a salary, health insurance, and paid time off. Remember, no one will totally get away with being crafty without eventually getting arrested, pay enormous fines and get several years of jail time. Incarceration is not an attractive look for any men who are attracted to the same sex to experience!

On Being Crafty
SIMC Rule 405

What sentence(s) in this rule stands out for you?

How would you define this rule for your social media followers?

On Getting in Them: Drags and Trannys
SIMC Rule 406

Implied throughout the rules is that men who are attracted to the same sex fall under a wide spectrum of behavior. Within the spectrum labels are assigned, like fem queen or butch queen or a piece of trade, etc. SIMC rule no. 406 discusses the specialized category of MAMs who are what is described as drag queens and transvestites /transgender (trannys). As a drag or tranny, you are a part of the MAM spectrum because of what you have in common with other men who are attracted to the same sex. The commonality is that many of you use your penis sexually, and you have no desire to have it removed. Where drags and trannys differ from other men who are attracted to the same sex, it is that you enjoy publicly displaying the illusion of the female standard of beauty. Other drag and tranny commonalities include competing in performance art, like lip-sync contests or walking in the ballrooms. If you are a part of this group, you enjoy wearing makeup, paint/powder, wigs, weaves, and panty hose, just to name a few. Before getting in them, you make sure you have on hand one of the secret weapons of drag—hairspray. Liquid foundation and blending the contours, along with other accoutrements, are all you need to make magic.

While drags and trannys have many similarities, there are subtle differences between the two groups. Chances are, if you are a real tranny, then you are on some sort of hormone therapy with a little cosmetic surgery thrown in for good measure. This is known as having moans and cones! In other words, your tits are real, your mug is "unclockable", and you live most of your day-to-day life as a male who appears female. As a drag queen, you have the unique ability to move between both worlds—a man by day and looking female when the occasion calls for it.

Becoming a drag queen allows certain MAMs the opportunity to show an inner core publicly. However, at the same time, there is something about displaying who you are as a male that you cling to as well. By getting in them, the irony is that you feel a masculine power while publicly embracing your own femininity. The bottom line is that the difference between the drag queen and the tranny boils down to tits that stay on and tits that can be removed!

Given what drag queens and trannys endure, the rules state that you are the bravest MAMs of all! This declaration can be established because you decided sometime as early as the neophyte stage to display your true self. There is an inner strength inside of you; it does not matter whether you are living in an urban housing project or in small town USA, with one Main Street. This strength had to be called upon while growing up because unlike other MAMs, you literally had to fistfight your way through those small towns or the school yards or the farmlands or the neighborhood streets.

Did you know that drags and trannys are the true athletes in the community of men who are attracted to the same sex? There are few professional athletes that can endure what you go through on a day-to-day basis. Think about it: getting in them and providing the illusion takes a lot of work. Imagine shaving, in some cases, more than twice daily, or think about beating your mug with grease paint and powder to give drama to your entrance and draw attention to your face. Think about choosing and styling the right hair so that it matched your total "effect." To complete that "effect" is no joke either; some say it takes a village to dress a drag queen!

In addition, getting in them includes rituals, like duct tape application, using Saran wrap, and even female undergarments. Then there is the ritual of using furniture cushions to create the precise hips, tits, asses, and thighs.

If that is not enough, the perfect outfit must not only stand out, but it must flatter your figure, as well as your skin tone. The ability to master the art of walking and performing in high heels are some of what it takes "to get in them." One more thing: getting in drags requires that you learn the art of tucking. This ritual means taking your penis carefully, pulling it toward the buttocks to hide any "loose change" so that you are giving the effect of female camel toe!

The bottom line is you have to respect what drag queens and trannys go through to provide magic through the art of illusion. The technique of being a drag or tranny does not happen overnight; it is learned through trial and error. These are the reasons why you sit on top of the heap. After all, it was drag queen self-determination that stood up to emotional and physical violence during Stonewall. As a matter of fact, your struggle ushered in the civil rights that exist for all MAMs today. Through it all, you have turned your scars into a birth right to be reckoned with!

Drag queens and trannys should not be confused with a transsexual.

Transsexuals are not a part of the MAM spectrum because this group, although they were born male in their core, is in the wrong gender. Most male-born transsexuals live their entire lives as females; it's purely brain chemistry. This group, in many cases, has applied for sexual reassignment surgery so that they can permanently change from male to female. Transsexual issues are complex and have nothing to do with homosexuality. One more note, cross-dressing is a fetish that has to do with heterosexual behavior and should be not be considered a part of the MAM spectrum as well.

On Getting in Them: Drags and Trannys
SIMC Rule 406

What sentence(s) in this rule stands out for you?

How would you define this rule for your social media followers?

What Is a MITCH, Bisexuality, MCM, and Understanding the Maydar Factor
SIMC Rule 407

The rules define men who are bisexual and exclusively attracted to drags and trannys as a MITCH. A MITCH is the male version of the sexual role he plays with drags and trannys. A true MITCH is visually attracted to the female illusion with the male parts attached. This subset on the spectrum derives pleasure by enjoying same-sex freedom with drag queens and trannys exclusively. If you are a MITCH, then your secret feelings for these types of MAMs began as early as the neophyte stage. Sexual arousal occurs when you are in the company of a male who looks like a female. There is a natural curiosity to experience sexual pleasures from a female look-alike with a penis. No wonder as a MITCH, you will not sexually associate with other MAMs who do not meet your fantasy criteria. Psychology, for you, is the combination of the visual and the tactile sensations that only a drag or tranny can fulfill.

A MITCH, in most cases, sees drags and trannys as an extension of his female relationships but with a twist! There are some in this subset who will engage in sexual role play by being the submissive one during sexual encounters.

What Is a MITCH, Bisexuality, MCM, and Understanding the Maydar Factor
SIMC Rule 407

What sentence(s) in this rule stands out for you?

How would you define this rule for your social media followers?

Bisexuality
SIMC Rule 407B

While most MITCHs are bisexual, only a few bisexuals are MITCHs. Also, some men on the low are bisexual, but not all bisexuals are on the low in the true sense of the term. The average bisexual is a MAM who enjoys the social and sexual pleasures of both genders. When you are bisexual, you know what you want; you have the freedom to choose the gender you find attractive at the time. For you, there are distinct differences between a man and a woman sexually. Bisexuals have the ability to enjoy both males and females because each gender has different physical and emotional sensations. As a bisexual, you are the least discriminating of all MAMs. Some may be attracted to closeted men so that your life remains separate for the larger same-sex community. By the same token, others may be attracted to men who have a feminine quality. Then there's a segment of you who are turned on just by another MAM's style and how he carries himself in public.

Mostly, many bisexuals live life as a heterosexual man within family relationships and in front of the public. While there is a conflict you may grapple with from time to time, all in all, you manage to live your life on your terms. Bisexuals have patience; you take your time with the choices you make. You know how to establish limits on what you can and cannot have from each gender. For you, it's all about the timing. There is a myth that you are confused because you have attraction to both males and females at the same time; frankly, for many bisexuals, this is not the case.

Innately, you have an overwhelming need to share your love, and there are times when one gender cannot fill your sensual gratification. This kind of attraction is not publicly spoken about in general conversation. If you are in a relationship with a female or male, your attraction is not a guilty pleasure. Bisexuals are able to rationalize this thought because for you, being with a man is not equal to cheating with another woman or vice versa. Face it, being attracted to both sexes is a complicated process. If you are attracted to bisexuals, you have to fundamentally understand that you are sharing him with a female; social-cultural demands say there are times she will come first in his public life. Therefore, try to avoid manipulating the situation to turn out in your favor. If you do so, he may flee. Understand his right to self-determination by allowing him to make the decisions about what gender comes first in his life. Remember, bisexuality is a real natural part of the being attracted to the same sex.

Contained within the wide spectrum of MAMs is a phenomenon called biquestioning. This is a male who will think about or is curious concerning what is happening inside of him because from time to time, he may experience same sex feelings. What separates you from a bisexual is that in many cases, physically being with another male is rarely acted upon. This curious sexual desire does not happen with all men you encounter. If you are biquestioning every now and then throughout your life at times, there are only a few males whom you find attractive. Not every male will bring up these feelings for you. On this spectrum, you may go through your entire life without acting out these feelings, or you may rarely, on occasion, act out the thought. This is key to what makes you biquestioning. When you are with someone who is biquestioning, then you must allow him to initiate the terms of the intimate exchange when and if he's ready.

Bisexuality
SIMC Rule 407B

What sentence(s) in this rule stands out for you?

How would you define this rule for your social media followers?

MCM
SIMC Rule 407C

An MCM is a heterosexual male who is so comfortable and secure in his manhood that he has the ability to be publicly close friends with men who are attracted to the same sex without prejudice, judgment, or bias. He could be your neighbor, distant family member, or friend who takes the time to make you a part of his world and you can discuss your world with him. He may not hang out with you every day, but he is always supportive.

An MCM can show up during the different stages in your life. When you're a neophyte, the MCM will be the peer who steps up for you when you are being bullied. During the ingénue, supernova, ikonoclass, and legacy stages, the MCM is your carpool passenger or train buddy or your gym partner. At times, he is the friend who you watch sports with or you go out with for cocktails or coffee. The MCM may be your coworker, or your neighbor. You are invited to his weddings and parties, and you may even have a relationship with his wife and children. He is a male who is comfortable enough in his manhood that no matter how much his heterosexual buddies tease him or his family may not understand the relationship, he remains by your side in a platonic way.

It is important to understand that this is a relationship that should be treasured and never be taken for granted. Therefore, many agree that it is not permitted to create conflict in your relationship by crossing sexual boundaries with your MCM. Keep in mind: it is a myth for men who are attracted to the same sex to think that you can seduce a true heterosexual male into experimenting sex with the same gender.

MCM
SIMC Rule 407C

What sentence(s) in this rule stands out for you?

How would you define this rule for your social media followers?

Understanding the May-dar Factor
SIMC Rule 407D

As a MAM, you should always be able to know when you are in the presence of another like-minded soul. There is a kind of natural sixth sense that forces you to recognize other men who are also attracted to the same sex. This recognition occurs no matter how much he may camouflage his true sexuality. The May-dar factor is an internal compass so powerful that you know when someone else is like you just by either looking at his photograph or hearing his conversation or watching his body language. When another MAM is in the room, you hone into how he may walk or talk. Furthermore, ultimately you pay attention, not to what he says around others but to what he is not saying. The rules here is never doubt your ability to see other men through your May-dar factor. Usually, this sixth sense will never steer you in the wrong direction.

In addition, using May-dar, knowing another man who is attracted to the same sex is in the room does not mean that you should equate this realization with mutual attraction. To approach or "push up on" a stranger because your May-dar says he is attracted to the same sex can be very dicey; you may not be his type. This is especially important if you are a MAM who has a difficult time with rejection!

Understanding the May-dar Factor
SIMC Rule 407D

What sentence(s) in this rule stands out for you?

How would you define this rule for your social media followers?

The Relationship Components, Marriage, and When Love Leaves
SIMC Rule 408

The healthy MAM relationship in many cases consists of special components for 100 percent sustainability. The rules suggest if any of these percentages add or subtract from the total of the formula, then both of you may want to recreate a balance. The formula includes:

20 percent respectful commitment and understanding him;

30 percent healthy communication and understanding who you are; and

50 percent emotional compatibility and sexual passion.

These percentages illustrate that a committed relationship between the two of you should have blended and expanded on the above components. In many cases, MAMs establish an unwritten contract with one another; it is unique within each relationship. When you are ready to open your life to a long-term commitment, it makes sense that you have worked on yourself first. After you've been emotionally centered, there are primary questions to answer. Have you agreed to accept each other's perfections as well as the imperfections? Have the two of you created an unwritten relationship contract? If you answer yes to these questions, then you're on the road to a respectful commitment. It means that you are devoted to each other even on those days you are pissed off with him!

When you've recognized that you cannot control or change each other's behavior, thoughts, or feelings, you begin to understand him.

Just because you understand him does not mean each time there are negative issues in the relationship, you have to behave appropriately because you made a commitment. Hey, you're human; it's very cathartic to get a little emotional. Just don't stay there too long.

Healthy communication means that you have come to the realization that there are three points of view to every difficult situation. There is his point; there is your point; and there is the truth. By the way, the truth always reveals itself eventually. When these bumps occur in relationships, you must stop, look, but most of all, actively listen. Active listening is hearing not just what's being spoken but paying attention to his body language, personality traits, habits, and what he is not saying. When you create a goal to actively listen, healthy communication can be actualized.

While you are in a committed relationship, you may choose to work on individual goals independent of him. When you begin to maintain individuality in the relationship, you own who you are inside and outside of the union. The point is this formula cannot work unless you understand who you are and what your role is with him.

Then there's intimacy; it is a spiritual yet sensual energy that you feel for each other before sex actually happens. In other words, intimacy is a part of being emotionally compatible. Intimacy is a kind of energy that compels you to join in a committed relationship. It is very natural that an element of intimacy includes *physical passion*. Power, being in charge, or controlling the situation is what you intrinsically have in common with all males.

There is a sense that a male power dynamic exists no matter how masculine or feminine you behave. Allowing intimacy is the act of displaying your confidence, as well as your insecurities with him. In fact, you may feel vulnerable when you perceive that you've turned over power to another male. That's a big deal!

Intimacy is important, but in the final analysis, carnal passion, along with mutual sexual gratification, looms largely in a committed relationship with him. The rules advise you to know your own erogenous self before you allow each other to make love. Creating sexual passion during love making should never become routine with your partner. Keep in mind: there is always another level for two males to achieve sexually. True same-sex love making, if done correctly, is an art form. If you are good between the sheets, then this action will leave a lasting impression, even when you are not around! As the relationship becomes more seasoned, your sexual passion and openness must continue to evolve.

The Relationship Components, Marriage, and When Love Leaves
SIMC Rule 408

What sentence(s) in this rule stands out for you?

How would you define this rule for your social media followers?

On Marriage
SIMC Rule 408B

When the two of you mix the right formula together, now you are ready to declare your love in front of family, friends, and the state. In other words, you want what most citizens want when love is declared, and that is to get married. Prior to the Supreme Court decision the rules always supportted marriage equality and the removal of DOMA in all fifty states and the U.S. territories as well. Marriage equality means that as a man who is attracted to the same sex, he should have the rights that heterosexuals enjoyed for centuries. The right for you and him to legally make a commitment in front of the state and even federal government is a no brainer! According to many studies, the difference between someone who is legally married compared to someone in a domestic partnership or common law marriage is vast. There are more than a thousand laws in this country that married couples enjoy, no matter what state they reside.

In 2013, the conservative supreme court, as they say, snatched everyone's faces when they ordered DOMA removed in the states where marriage equality is legal. Their California Proposition 8 decision made a third of the nation a place where same-sex marriage is also federal law. The struggle continues; there's a tough fight ahead, but make no mistakes. You should have the fight anyway. It's important to remember change is not something that occurs in this society overnight. Discrimination concerning interracial marriage was against the law in this country until California became the first state to recognize these unions in the late 1940s. However, it took another twenty years before White Americans and Black Americans could marry each other within all fifty states.

Given this fact, the question becomes how do we prepare against bias and homophobia that will more than likely follow once marriage equality is achieved? Is it accomplished state by state or on a federal level?

Once you've achieved equal status, as an MAM, you should think about how your marriage ceremony should look differently. Equality should not be confused with assimilation; marriage between two men should not look like a heterosexual one, or maybe it should?

On Marriage
SIMC Rule 408B

What sentence(s) in this rule stands out for you?

How would you define this rule for your social media followers?

When Loves Leaves
SIMC Rule 408C

There are times, despite your best efforts, when what you thought you had with him did not stand the test of time. When you first met him, one of three events may have happened. Was it love at first sight, or maybe he loved you before you realized it? Was it because as time went by you went from a platonic friendship to passionate lovers? When love leaves, what attracted you to him is less important than the alienation of affection which contributed to the breakup. Committed relationships end long before the physical act of leaving occurs. Some of the questions you think about when love leaves are: *Was it my fault? Was it something I said? Was it something that I've done? What's wrong with me?* Then there are those of you who think about your breakup in a sort of narcissistic way, for example: *He lied to me; he hurt me, and I will never trust him again! I was the best lover he will ever have. He's going to pay for how he treated me!* Then there are those who may have other responses to this situation. The point is, when you find out that it's not forever, you feel it on an emotional level.

If you are thinking about being the first to leave, the ultimate question is how do you know when to walk away? The rules suggest if the relationship is not feeding your soul, then you should think about an exit strategy! When you've reached the point in your relationship where trust is threatened, there are certain decisions you have to make. When to break up is an individual choice. In many cases, before this action happens, you must not only weigh what you hear and what you perceive, but how you feel plays a significant role as well.

If you choose to discuss the intent to break up with him, then be aware of the message you are sending. It's smart to clearly say what you mean and mean what you say! The next decision you make is gather the facts and know the answers to your own questions first. Once you've done these things, you are ready to deal with any potential conflict effectively.

There are many dramatic episodes in what the rules call the backwater blues. The backwater blues are those stressful times in a relationship when both of you chose to ignore the hurt inflected on one another. In other words, the argument is never resolved. When this occurs, you stuff hurt feelings inside, and then the two of you act as if nothing happened. This pattern repeats itself until one day, one of you walks. It is natural to have your own deal breaker when it comes to setting limits within your relationship. If cheating is an issue, try not to fall into the trap of blaming a third party. The burden of cheating is the relationships' responsibility, not the one on the outside.

In the end or in the beginning, it depends on how you want to look at it; unless the breakup was mutual, leaving someone physically and emotionally is a transformative moment for both of you. The healthy action to take when a love leaves is to cry it out, find a distraction, talk about it, self-reflect, dust yourself off, and get back into the race! After he leaves, be aware that grieving over a relationship for more than a few months can at times cause you to go from sadness to a depressive episode. Once depression occurs, seeking therapy or even taking a prescribed antidepressant is warranted. Consult a psychiatrist. Therapy from a licensed clinical social worker or psychologist is a good first step as well. One more thing to consider, when it's newly over, you may want to stay away from asking to remain friends. Instead, consider allowing the friendship to evolve or not evolve naturally, without your interference.

When Loves Leaves
SIMC Rule 408C

What sentence(s) in this rule stands out for you?

How would you define this rule for your social media followers?

Domestic Violence
SIMC Rule 408D

Domestic violence (DV) among some men who attracted to the same sex is a reality. In many cases, these dangerous acts have to do with certain emotional health issues or lack of coping skills. Rule of thumb: when it comes to domestic violence, you should think critically. Love should not emotionally or physically hurt! If he physically makes you feel unsafe, then you are in a domestic violence situation. If he verbally or emotional abuses you frequently and you're walking on eggshells, then you are in a domestic violence situation. For some males, to publicly state another male is hurting you may invite feelings of shame and ridicule. Don't be afraid; this is your very life. Get up, get help, and get out of that relationship! No matter how much he makes it up to you after the first DV act, statistics state he will hurt you again.

Eventually, with support, there comes a time when you decide you can't live together. If it's your home, be prepared for the drama. This means declaring the abuse publicly because you will either use the legal system or you call on your CFFs. By the way, removing him from your home should always be done within the law. Afterward, make sure you file for an order of protection. Don't be afraid to contact your local police as well. Creating a paper trail in domestic violence cases is your mission. If you are walking away, then be prepared to leave everything there and get out when he least expects it.

Keep in mind that material things are replaceable; you have but one life! It is assured that if you make a change, you will live through it and come out on the other side, stronger. Check within your local community about same-sex domestic violence services, including the local district attorney's office. If there aren't any services where you live, then start one. Demand equal protection rights. Research the laws of your state and see what federal statutes can help too. Domestic violence stops when men like you take action to safely and lawfully end it!

Domestic Violence
SIMC Rule 408D

What sentence(s) in this rule stands out for you?

How would you define this rule for your social media followers?

Online Activity, Cruising, the Rambles, Tea Rooms, and Person to Person
SIMC Rule 409

Online dating has become a common practice in today's culture. This fact is also true for men who are attracted to the same sex. Looking for Mr. Right or Mr. Right Now on social media has become a rite of passage for MAMs. Today, by the time you reach the ingénue stage, you are in most cases trying your first adult experience with online dating. The term *online dating* for many men who are attracted to the same sex can be an oxymoron. On Web sites, with names like *Adam4 Adam, Man Hunt, Craigslist, Grindr,* or others, there is little dating and more hooking up for sex. These websites have become a place where many men who are attracted to the same sex meet. The allure of these sites is that they are designed to state what you want without the awkwardness of the face-to-face contact. Despite this fact, many will agree online dating can be an enjoyable experience for some men who are attracted to the same sex.

In the pursuit of the conquest, there are a number of you who use the cover of Web sites to not be forthcoming about your real physical appearance or sexual prowess. According to the rules, when you decide to join a dating web site, it's always a good thing to be as accurate as possible. This applies to what you look like and what you are into sexually. This rule includes stating your real age, a shocking concept for sure! Just because you don't look your age, he will soon discover that you are older or younger than the age on your profile. The giveaway to how old you are has to do with your physical appearance, your conversation, and what you are interested in.

This perception includes your frame of reference or even how your home is decorated. Never confuse his youth or his advanced age for that matter as naivety! When you allow website members to know your real statistics, an informed decision can be made by the other party. Therefore, when the hookup happens, there are no misconceptions. The thing to remember is that eventually you will meet the other guy, and his reaction to you will be based on what you stated in the Web site.

Okay, so you are ready to cruise the Web site and you hit up the screen name Johnny who lives across town. *Johnny's stats states that he is twenty-eight years old, slim, stands six feet two, weighs 195 pounds. He has long dark hair, he's a top, and he has a nine-inch dick, thick cut. After several back-and-forth messages, you are feeling sexually open, you decide to meet him, you're ready, and it's lit! Since he doesn't travel, you get in your car to go to his place. You arrive, and to your amazement, you find out he is more like forty-eight years old. He is six feet two, but it looks like the 195 pounds settled in his stomach, and his long dark hair begins where his receding hairline ends. Johnny "the Top" warmly greats you while wearing his tightest bikini underwear, leaving you to guess where the nine inches went and if you are really dealing with a top!*

Here are the decisions you ponder:

Do you go ahead with the date as planned and then make a quick exit before the sex begins?

Not wanting to hurt his feelings, do you stay, thinking maybe he's a grower and not a shower?

Then again, do you immediately turn away, run back to your car, and head home as fast as you can?

When setting up your online dating profile, make sure you clearly state your preferences. Once you have done so, if someone who did not read your profile hits you up, it's perfectly okay to ignore them or not. If you have an online stalker who does not get the message that you are not his type, then blocking him from contacting you is appropriate. If you are not clear about what you are looking for on the site, then don't send a nasty reply to the person who contacted you. When this happens, keep in mind that it's not his fault; it was you who was not clear.

Finally, many agree that it is important to state your true sexual role. When it comes to sex, as a MAM, you have several roles to choose from; make sure you declare your sexual role. Remember, there is nothing like arriving for an online date and finding out that you are not a match with the other person. The only fake thing on your online dating account should be your nom de guerre.

Online Activity, Cruising, the Rambles, Tea Rooms, and Person to Person
SIMC Rule 409

What sentence(s) in this rule stands out for you?

How would you define this rule for your social media followers?

On Cruising
SIMC Rule 409B

Cruising occurs when anytime you see another MAM and you attempt to make him aware of your interest by first using body language as a means of same-sex communication. The chemistry involved in how you communicate your interest to him is complicated. There are two main forms of cruising: one is cruising for sex, and the other is cruising for a relationship.

Let's look at cruising for sex. In the initial phase, the body language you use has to do with your eyes because they speak your intentions. Eye contact maybe the language used in the initial phase, but after that, there is another chemical reaction that happens. Without words, once eye contact is made, a sexual energy takes control. This feeling heightens your anxiety; it focuses you on making closer contact with the object of your cruise.

The next phase involves a more graphic form of body language. In most cases, there is a gesture, or he may point to a body part imploring you to follow him. To keep it real, blood pressures raise, adrenaline flows, and erections occur. At this point, still no words are yet spoken until you arrive at the secluded space where a brief conversation takes place. This is the process where the two of you stop for a five-minute meeting before anything physical occurs. Within that short time frame, you have found out all you need to know, including where both of you will go to perform the sexual act!

Cruising for a relationship in the beginning involves the same actions detailed in cruising for sex. The difference is when cruising for a relationship, the conversations are longer and dating commence. Both men really want to know each other. This interaction is more meaningful, and the eventual sex connection centers on the future as opposed to the here and now. When cruising, no matter what your intent, there is nothing like an old-fashioned face-to-face meeting in a public.

On Cruising
SIMC Rule 409B

What sentence(s) in this rule stands out for you?

How would you define this rule for your social media followers?

The Rambles and Tea Rooms
SIMC Rule 409C

Contained within small town USA to a big city, it's almost assured that rambles and tea rooms exist. Rambles and tea rooms are places where MAMs go to express themselves sexually while keeping anonymity. In other words, these are public cruising spots. Since the 1800s, a section of Central Park in New York City was given the name rambles; it was an isolated place in the middle of the largest city in the USA. It's one of the few green spaces where several large trees grew together. That area of the park was given its name by MAMs who frequented its secrets each night. This type of cruising has been done since a time when same-sex attraction was considered a crime. Today, "the rambles" is a name given to any city or state park where MAMs gather for sexual activity with each other. Large urban and rural park areas no matter where you live more than likely host ramble parties each night. How do you know about your town? These spots usually turn into the rambles at sundown . Check it out.

Tea room is the name given to any male public bathroom where sexual acts are preformed. This is a place where sex happens on the go. This time-honored tradition has been around as long as there have been public places where men gather. Today, even some gym locker rooms, gas stations, and truck stops have made a tea room revival. There are many men who are attracted to the same sex across the spectrum that has either a tea room story or stories about public sex. For some, this was the first sexual experience with another male. Tea rooms are also called the oral capital in the MAM world; it is considered a place where you're guaranteed good head!

Some say that performing a public sex act is abhorrent. Sex between two men should be conducted behind locked doors with the drapes drawn, at midnight, and out of public view!

When it comes to where you choose to have sex is your business. If you make a decision to perform this in public, then by all means do but know the law. At the end of the day, the rules recognize that same sex life allows for diversity; in this case, tea rooms, rambles, and the like are a part of what gratifies your inner sexual fantasy.

There are other public male institutions that no longer exist, but they played a huge role in MAM cruising history. Although several cruising establishments have become a part of the past, the rambles and tea rooms are perennial!

The Rambles and Tea Rooms
SIMC Rule 409C

What sentence(s) in this rule stands out for you?

How would you define this rule for your social media followers?

Person to Person
SIMC Rule 509D

The person-to-person meeting between men who are attracted to the same sex can happen almost anywhere. Today, even gyms and private jack parties have become a part of the MAM folklore as places where men can sexually interact with each other. There are several factors that come into play when meeting someone with whom you are attracted. Physical attributes is the primary factor awakened when you are attracted to another man for the first time. There is a myth that all MAMs are only attracted to perfect beauty and chiseled physiques. Those attributes are great ideals, but the truth is each of you has your own internal standards about who you find attractive. For many, height, weight, and knock-out looks aren't as important as his overall vibe, intelligence, and swagger. In other words, his overall manner has the ability to make you notice him in a crowd. Within a few minutes, you are observing how he handles himself in front of others. Like he is comfortable in public or maybe he is someone who is shy and unsure of himself; whatever he is, this turns you on! Even his appendages and how they are displayed publicly is another factor you include when it comes to attraction. For some, it is the way his penis lies through the imprint of his pants or how his buttocks is sitting just perfectly off his back that makes your erogenous zones react. His legs or thighs or arms or chest or even his nipples can be an attraction for you. Just as any heterosexual, appendages that can draw your attention are impossible to ignore.

Once the ideal comes along, it is at that point your imagination is free to fantasize. The fantasy may lasts for a few moments, and then your brain begins to strategize how to achieve the introductory conversation.

When two of these factors are in perfect balance, a connection has been made. You will know this because his conversations are authentic, and he is comfortable in his own skin. You recognize this because of the positive connection the two of you share during the exchange. Finally, the face-to-face meeting is a good way to remove many of the obstacles that newer forms of communications may have.

Person to Person
SIMC Rule 509D

What sentence(s) in this rule stands out for you?

How would you define this rule for your social media followers?

On Pastimes and Athleticisms
SIMC Rule 410

Since the beginning of organized society, music and drama has been a huge pastime for MAMs. The rules suggest that when cultures are repressed and hidden, they find a way to influence society without being obvious about their intent. Men who are attracted to the same sex mostly have a huge influence on pop culture genres today. In most cases, there are MAMs making the decisions about what you hear on the radio and see on the screen. Producers, directors, studio executives, super agents, and those who run pop culture have one thing in common with MAMs; many of them grew up with an innate instinct about the world and how colorful it could be. For example, what you wear and how you work the outfit can become trendy for the heterosexual population as well. The same goes for what you choose in classic Broadway musicals, dramatic movies, and even identifying the iconic popular singers.

One of the great pastimes for MAMs is to attend an entertaining musical production. The Broadway musicals have always been a part of the same-sex cultural experience. Even if you have not seen a live performance, chances are you have an affinity toward them. This is especially true for iconic musical productions. There is something about the great Broadway musicals which awaken the very soul of many men who are attracted to the same sex. It means that when you listen to music and lyrics of the great productions, you are inspired to keep moving forward in your own life. The rules focus on the foundation of this art form during the twentieth century. Here are some of the standards that future classic Broadway musicals will be judged:

Included on the small list of must-see musicals are:

Show Boat and the song, "Can't Help Loving Dat Man"
Porgy and Bess and the song "Summertime"
Oklahoma and the song "Oklahoma"
West Side Story
Dream Girls
The Wiz
Cabaret and the song "Cabaret"
Hair and the song "Hair"

A Chorus Line and the song "What I Did for Love"
La Cage aux Folles
Mame and the song "Bosom Buddies"

These productions, along with other unmentioned top favorites, are must-see events. On the other hand, there are other MAMs who were not exposed to musicals and may not have an appreciation for this phenomena; it's okay. The rules invite you to allow yourself permission to enjoy this art form known as great Broadway musical productions.

Another pastime for many MAMs is the appreciation for classic dramatic movies. Some say there are three elements a movie must have before it can be given the stamp of approval from MAMs. One element includes a great story line. A great story line must be a serious tearjerker or a sophisticated psychological thriller or of course, an over-the-top high-camp film. The second element needed is a witty, sincerely delivered dialogue that overall stimulates your senses. The rich structure of the conversations in the movie should awaken your aspirations while inspiring you at the same time. Finally, the actor must be able to deliver lines in an Oscar-nominated fashion!

Once all three elements appear on the screen, they are anointed with the blessings of MAMs. If you are a male who is attracted to the same sex, then you are advised to at look at what some will agree are the short list of must-see classic films. The list of a few must-see movies for MAMs include these iconic titles from the twentieth century.

The Little Foxes	*All About Eve*
Whatever Happened to Baby Jane	*The Women (1933)*
Flamingo Road	*Gone with the Wind*
Queen Bee	*Dodsworth*
Life Boat	*East of Eden*
Sunset Boulevard	*Cat on a Hot Tin Roof*
Backstreet	*Rope*
She Done Him Wrong	*The Roman Spring of Mrs. Stone*
The Rtiz	*Peyton Place*
Some Like It Hot	*Carmen*

Funny Girl   *John Waters' films*
The Valley of the Dolls   *The Children's Hour*
Victim   *Barbarella*
The Boys in the Band   *The Lion in the Winter*
The Sexette   *The Rocky Horror Picture Show*
Butch Cassidy and the Sundance Kid *Turning Point*
Making Love   *Mommie Dearest*
Torch Song Trilogy   *Lady Sings the Blues*
The Wiz   *Mahogany*

Movies with sports themes or film noir or superheroes are all genres that men who are attracted to the same sex enjoy as well. There are many other unmentioned movies produced in the past that had hidden or sometimes overt same-sex themes or appeal. The rules invite you to take a look at these films because they help you understand and appreciate the traditions you have today. Here's to the movies and its stars!

While Broadway musicals and classic movies may have helped shaped the culture we enjoy today, the invention of recorded sound to the masses was a game changer. When records became easily accessible, MAMs created music royalty especially among its female singers. Many of these women became superstars all achieving number 1 status on the charts. Before a female singer is exalted to iconic status, chances are she had a strong MAM following that placed her there. Men who are attracted to the same sex, like their heterosexual counterparts, can appreciate beautiful, feminine, sexy, well-dressed, and talented women. There are many other reasons why this attraction exists. But if you look around, the symbiotic relationships between these women and MAMs is evident.

The female singing star must have four key ingredients or the Ross recipe if you will in order to have a MAM following:

1. *A phenomenal talent, with more than a six top ten songs, who is comfortable in the studio and in front of a live band.*
2. *Possess exquisite style and have the influence to set fashion or other cultural trends by using her platform in a purpose-driven way to help others off stage as well.*

3. Be able to make a name for herself above the rest of her peers using her voice and award winning showmanship skills.
4. Younger singers may emulate her, but everyone knows she set the standard first.

Without those qualities, some say she cannot be considered iconic or music royalty. Here is one definitive list for a number of MAMs these women take their place in a rarefied strata called trailblazers. They have reached the level of iconic statues because of their more than twenty years on top of charts. *Judy G., Ella F., Nina S., Billie H., Sarah V., Lena H., Dinah W., The Andrew Sisters, Shirley B., Diana Ross, Barbra S., and Cher. Aretha, Dionne, Bette, Tina, Patti, and Gladys. Chaka, Liza, Martha W., Janet, Whitney, and Madonna.*

Of course, there are other iconic entertainers who have a real MAM following and now considered music royalty. Since the 1990s up until the present day, singers like *Celine, Mariah, Jennifer L., Beyonce, Jenifer H., Britney, Pink, Lt. Kim, Nikki, Rihanna, Katy, and Lady Gaga* are all on their way to royalty status in a few more years but not yet! There are several more unnamed great female vocalists or rappers today. Knowing the rules, who do you consider music royalty? What male singers would make your list as well?

On Pastimes and Athleticisms
SIMC Rule 410

What sentence(s) in this rule stands out for you?

How would you define this rule for your social media followers?

Athleticism
SIMC Rule 410B

Make no mistakes about it; athletic competitions and sporting events hold a special place for a number of MAMs. It's a huge myth to think that men who are attracted to the same sex do not share an affinity for team and individual sports just like their heterosexual counterparts. It could be a conference game, Super Bowl or playoff championship, NBA final, or even the World Series; men who are attracted to the same sex are there. We can't forget soccer's World Cup, the most-watched popular game on the planet. Representation of males who are attracted to the same sex extends to those participants who are a part of a sports franchise or as an individual player in a game. Athleticism is both a natural and a learned behavior that ignites a spirit of competition in the male psyche. This spirit has an appeal because winning, being the dominant one, is how most males were socialized. Highlighted in this rule is an alternative look into the top three athletic events that many American heterosexual men enjoy and many MAMs as well.

Beginning with the aggressive game of gladiators, it's one of the sports with a same-sex following. This is a game where two different teams employ offensive, defensive, and special team strategies to score points. One aspect of the game is to either get to the end zone or prevent the other team from getting there. This game is about the thrill of battle, punctuated with words like yardage, wide receiver, tight end, fullback, and the forward pass. In addition, there's the subliminal interaction between the center and quarterback that catches your attention.

The game is called football; it's where modern gladiators score points while being chased by several men, many of whom are trying to catch your backfield in motion.

If he's caught making a pass or gaining yardage, the guys on the other team will forcefully grab him and make him go down! According to the rules, football is an engaging athletic orgy of male aggression and organized sadomasochism while holding on to a brown ball.

Another popular game can best be described as a royal court where physically graceful gazelles walk on air—no other team sport can match this feat without man-made assistance. The players in this game are mostly tall, sometimes small, skillful, stealthy, and athletically coordinated. Five men from each team hold court while sprinting fast and jumping high to score points. Basketball, the sport that hits the sweet spot is the name of this game. There is a pure animalistic intimacy that occurs when this game is played. It starts with the fact that they pair up in couples on the court, and each play can turn into a duo or a threesome depending on who's holding the ball. Basketball players have positions like point guards, shooting guards, centers, power forwards, and small forwards all on the rebound! The emotional highs and lows that occur when these gazelles hit a shot from downtown are thrilling. There is an excitement that is felt deeply when a player scores points by touching a big ball and slamming it into a round-netted hole! Anticipation builds when he has a foul or is caught holding another player the wrong way. There are times when a shot clock violation occurs; after that, the game gets particularly interesting. When the game is coming to a close, testosterone goes up, causing bodies to sweat with pure animalistic adrenaline.

They release you when the game is over, establishing who's on top and who's in the bottom position. The rules note that watching this game can be a sensual, rhythmic, voyeuristic adventure. Basketball is pure male frottage, a game designed for hand-and-body contact while wearing tank tops and shorts!

Baseball is a popular sport in the USA and other countries. There are many MAMs who enjoy this game known as America's pastime. Some may argue that of all the team sports, baseball, the game of gloves, bats, and balls, is the least sensual. However, this pastime has its own language and customs. In baseball, men gather together in a dugout. They deal with innings, touch bases, and play with long hard wooden bats. In this game, there are not only pitchers, but there are also catchers, and both can slide into home base. The rules explain that this pastime is about manipulating little balls, getting tagged, and hitting a home run. If these few examples did not open your eyes to get into team sports, then consider this: *penetration* is a term used in both football and basketball. In addition, no matter what team sport is played, there's just one way to congratulate each other—that's with a pat on the ass! So the next time one of your heterosexual friends, family, or coworker asks you to watch a game, you'll be able to watch it through a different worldview.

Finally, there are the sports of individual competitive endurance, like track, swimming, and tennis. There is a natural instinct for some MAMs to participate in and enjoy sports that displays single accomplishments too. Many suggest that before Gay Pride parades existed, events like the Penn Relays, the U.S. Open and other track and field events were places where MAMs gathered to meet like-minded individuals.

Athleticism
SIMC 410B

What sentence(s) in this rule stands out for you?

How would you define this rule for your social media followers?

The Rules on Sex and Sexuality
The SS Rules 500–510

Male sexuality is an extremely complicated phenomenon, and it can be very difficult to describe. There are those who argue that men are first attracted to each other sexually long before an emotional commitment is established. The subject of men and sexuality is far too vast for just one chapter in one book. Therefore, the rules in this chapter will provide you with a brief blueprint about the subject. That way, you can use your own curiosity to navigate this important facet of who you are sexually. The first thing to remember is that you are not defined by how much sex you can engage in. Copulation is important, but intimacy, companionship, and friendship are even more crucial. With that said, the sex and sexuality or SS rules will look at just a few aspects about sexual habits and other erotic themes.

This chapter begins with the rules concerning the most important and celebrated body part in the male anatomy, the penis. The penis and the power of this organ loom largely, not only in MAM culture but in all society. In ancient Greece and Rome, one of their deities who presided over good fortune during travels was Priapus; he was usually placed outside of a person's home. The statue's most unique feature was its large penis which visitors rubbed for safe journeys.

Today, if a man has been diagnosed with priapism, then it means his penis has been permanently erect for several hours. The rules invite you to get know the penis, learn to appreciate it, no matter how many inches you possess. It's the realization that this organ is a major area where male power is derived.

This notion should empower you to internalize that when comparing yourself to other males, try to think to yourself: *I will win because I've got the biggest dick in the room!* Embracing this mantra means having the confidence about who you are as a strong male figure and a sexual being. The penis is not only responsible for creating life, but it is also the force that controls life once it arrives. In this chapter, the rules describe the definition of this exclusively male organ and the science of its functions. Masturbation is also discussed, along with new descriptions about penis performance called i-dic-ta-fi-cation.

Another rule concerns itself with oral stimulation and the sexual power attained if you master this skill. There are rules written covering the buttocks, its biological functions, along with how to keep it sexually clean and healthy. In the section about intercourse, this rule provides examples of different sexual positions by assigning new definitions to a few of them.

The sex and sexuality rules shed light on the meaning of some of today's MAM popular sexual labels. Role descriptions like oral tops, power bottoms, and true meaning of versatility are discussed. Safe sex, how to perform it, and how to achieve it is also covered in this chapter. In addition, sexual involvement outside of traditional couple dynamic is explored. Finally, included in this chapter is information concerning risky behavior, the what, the when, the where, and the how, including the reasons why you may want to avoid it. Let's begin!

The Penis a.k.a. Your Johnson
SS Rule 501

Penis is an old Latin word meaning tail. Cut or uncut, the penis is an external male extremity that has three main parts. It functions as an organ of the body where both urine and semen pass. Then there's a prostate gland, and rounding out the three are the testicles. One of its functions as a major organ aside from depositing urine happens when the penis becomes erect or hard. Furthermore, the rules say ejaculation can only occur if the penis is stimulated by four physical acts. They are identified as hand stimulation, oral stimulation, anal intercourse, and/or vaginal intercourse.

Both pre-cum and semen are carried through tube-shaped gland called the prostate. The prostate is a pecan size object that is located in front of the anus and behind the bladder. There are times when, for some, this gland can be stimulated through the anus during sex.

The third extremity is called the testicles; it is solid in two halves, and it's located under the penis. The testicles are like an incubator for male sperm. One ejaculation releases hundreds of millions of little swimmers which are all contained in the scrotum. The scrotum is the sac that holds the pecan-size testis. The scrotum keeps sperm above freezing but not too warm, which is what medical evidence states is the ideal temperature to produce big shooters!

The power of this male organ is not a new phenomenon; the penis and its mythology have been celebrated throughout prehistory.

The ancient Egyptians told the story of one of their male deities who was mortally wounded. His wife, the queen, escorted him down the Nile River to the underworld. During the journey, she climbed on top of his erection and was impregnated. The story suggests that the ability to procreate, combined with the addictive nature of the organ, makes the phallus powerful indeed. Since the beginning of human civilization, some men have used penis power to gain popularity, influence in governments, and attain social control. There's a segment of heterosexual men who are able to use this power effectively. These men do so partly because they've tapped into the confidence of how they feel about their penis. It's the fear of this power that have caused women, people of color, and the same-sex community to step aside, while these men make laws restricting equality. As an MAM, think about taking back your authority by realizing your own penis power. This power is not only about the phallus you have, but it's about the confidence you feel about yours.

The rules suggest that you should get to know your penis, learn how to feel confident about the manhood between your legs. Every now and then, it's perfectly okay to admire your penis. You only have one; find out what feels good to it. Once you've gone through this process, you are now ready to enjoy masturbation or jerking off.

There is nothing more healthy than this frequent form of sex enjoyed by almost all human beings. Masturbation is the one of the safest forms of sex, and you can continue this act well into your golden legacy years. Masturbation allows you to safely explore your fantasies which are at times more satisfying than reality. However, you do have to live in reality; there are some of you who believe that when it comes to the penis, size does matter.

Research literature suggests that in America, cut or uncut, the average penis size is about seven inches erect. This leads to the age-old question: is it about the size of the ship or the motion in the ocean? For some, if you were in an ocean, a large ship is a good thing. Then there are those who say that motion in the ocean can bring you closer together and more often. The rules encourage you to conduct your own research on the topic. Always seek more information!

The Penis a.k.a. Your Johnson
SS Rule 501

What sentence(s) in this rule stands out for you?

How would you define this rule for your social media followers?

I-dic-ta-fi-cation
SS Rule 501B

There is a population of men who have described the penis with names like your dick or your package or your basket or your Johnson. However, many of you assign names according to length and width. The rules identify four types of penises as it relates to length, width, and more importantly, how it functions. They are: the IED or the intermediate explosive device; the LRM or the long-range missile; the WMD or the weapon of mass destruction; and the SM or the scud missile.

Let's look at the IED, the intermediate explosive device. The IED is described as an average-size penis, but what it lacks is size; it makes up for the sexual pleasure it provides. If you have an IED, then you are able to make him feel like the only goal when the two of you make love is sexual satisfaction! IEDs have the ability to hit the right spot instinctively, and it doesn't explode until you are ready. The IED, when erect, can indeed be a powerful weapon inside and outside of the bedroom.

The second type describes a penis that, length wise, is more than average size. LRM or long-range missile, some say, is the most popular kind of penis. It is said that LRMs can be so good sexually that it becomes addictive. One key feature of having an LRM is that you are a big shooter. In other words, your ejaculations are legendary! This kind of penis will make you travel across the country, take time from work, or maybe even empty your bank account! It's the penis you dream about long after the sex act is done.

If you have the weapon of mass distraction or WMD, then your penis is unusually large and impressive. You literally do have the biggest dick in the room, and everyone wants a chance to make it erect. The WMD is the penis most sought after for many of you who like to engage in oral pleasure. When it comes to anal sex, this penis can enlarge your sphincter muscle and make you feel it in your prostate gland! The art of taking a WMD has to do with the sexual position; it is recommended that you and your partner find a way that's comfortable. If you have the skills and know what you are doing, then the WMD is the penis for you.

Last but not least is the scud missile or SM. The SM has nothing to do with penis size, but it has more to do with performance. If you are walking around with an SM, then no matter what size penis you have, the rules surmise at best you're sexually boring, or at worst, you're being selfish. Either you have difficulty getting fully erect, or you cum too quickly, or your love making skills are lacking. How do you know you have an SM? Sexually, your partners never come back for more!

I-dic-ta-fi-cation
No. 501B

What sentence(s) in this rule stands out for you?

How would you define this rule for your social media followers?

Fellatio a.k.a. Giving Head
SS Rule 502

One of the most frequent enjoyed sexual activities for a MAM is fellatio—that neck or head. Fellatio means that the penis is orally stimulated, causing it to become erect, eventually ejaculating semen or cum or nut. There is an unspoken understanding before most MAMs are sexually intimate; fellatio will be a part of the equation. When it comes to pleasing your partner, how good you are at performing this basic sexual act can be the difference between feast and famine! Just like many forms of sexual activity, if fellatio is done according to the natural flow, then both of you should be stimulated. The best head is achieved by first psychologically acknowledging an oral fixation for this activity. One way to prepare is to have the curiosity to give or receive head. Furthermore, the act itself must turn you on. Skill development in this area comes with time and experience; you don't have to be *deep throat*, but you must know what you are doing. If you are new at it, try not to be in a situation where you are rushed. Take the time to use your entire mouth to slowly explore his trade. Keep in mind: even those who give the best head had to start from somewhere.

There are few steps the rules will share concerning how to perform fellatio. One is that both the stimulator and the one being stimulated must be prepared for the act. This means you may want to try foreplay prior to the oral act. This is accomplished by gently touching the penis firm yet masculine while you are both still clothed. Foreplay could include kissing, nipple action, or even simulating and pulling his head to your crotch area.

If done correctly, at this point, both of you should be erect. Tongue, mouth, and lips exploration is advised for the prefellatio experience. Use it to explore his erogenous zones. These zones are different for each individual; what turns you on may not turn him on. Some may want the scrotum or balls gently caressed; others may not.

On the other hand, his silent gestures or verbal commands will let you know how far you can go with the pre-oral exploration. When his penis is in your mouth and if you have to use your hands too much, you may not be turning him on.

The rest is up to you. No one can really tell how to give head; it just has to feel good to him and be good for you.

Fellatio a.k.a. Giving Head
SS Rule 502

What sentence(s) in this rule stands out for you?

How would you define this rule for your social media followers?

Head Positions
SS Rule 502B

There are many fellatio positions you can get into as a MAM. The rules invite you to take a look at three. One position is called knee padding; this happens when you kneel to provide head while he is standing. If knee padding is a favorite position for you, the rules caution you to invest in pads or pillows; protect your knees at all cost! Of course, if you are in a rambles or tea room, it's advised that you find a toilet or tree stump or rock to sit down on. Keep in mind: the important thing is to be creative while performing knee padding in a public place.

Another position is called double duty; it occurs when both of you are serving head to each other. Unlike 69, a heterosexual label, double duty reflects the reality that this is an act that only males can perform on each other simultaneously. For males, this act is more like a 99 than the old label. The fellatio position can occur when you are side by side or when your bodies face each other from opposite ends. During double duty, when it comes to ejaculation, one of you may release or ejaculate before the other. It is rare that both of you will cum in the same moment while performing this act, so practice patience.

The last of the top three positions is called oral copulation. This act occurs when you lie on your back, allowing him to startle you while he simulates sex by thrusting the penis in and out of your mouth. If preformed with the right rhythm, then oral copulation should inspire you to gingerly grab his posterior and jerk your own hard erection simultaneously.

No matter which position you try, this should be a private agreement between you and your partner(s). Even the decision where semen should be ejaculated rests in the hands of both of you, no pun intended.

Semen can be ejaculated on his ass, chest, or face, and then there are some who don't like it near them at all. If you want to ingest or swallow semen, enjoy it, but watch out. While oral sex has been found to have low risk for sexually transmitted disease, any exchange of bodily fluids can be a risky choice. If a wound or cut or sore is in the area, then the chances of contracting STDs increase. As a MAM, you should have a fellatio style and always remember to watch the teeth when performing this act!

Head Positions
SS Rule 502B

What sentence(s) in this rule stands out for you?

How would you define this rule for your social media followers?

The Gluteus Maximus a.k.a. The Booty
SS Rule 503

The gluteus maximus or buttocks or booty is the largest of three muscles located on the back of a human's body. It is an enhancement to your overall shape and can be a very prominent part of your physique. In sports, the gluteus is the dominant muscle used for football, volleyball, basketball, soccer, and hockey. The buttocks (gluteus), the anus, and the sphincter make up the muscles found on the back of your body. One of the most important aspects of the buttocks is that located in the center of it, there's an anus.

The anus has several functions; one is that it can act as a sexual organ. It is a sensitive area that is close to the prostate gland. There are nerve endings in the anus which can be reactive when stimulated. These nerves can be motivated by foreplay with nipple manipulation or oral contact or even by using a finger to gently rub around the outer edges of the anal cavity. Sometimes when the anus is stimulated, the prostate feels great pleasure, increasing the possibility of an ejaculation. However, if the anus is not either physically prepared or the person is not mentally ready, it can be painful or even make you feel like you need to urinate. The anus is surrounded by the sphincter muscle.

The sphincter muscle is the third part of the gluteus maximums; it is strong, contracting in and out during entrances and exists. When having anal sex, it is the sphincter that controls the penis inside of the anus.

When cleaned, relaxed, and well lubricated, it opens and closes depending on the rhythm of sexual penetration. The first time you lose what's called your booty virginity, there may be some slight discomfort. This is a natural occurrence. With time, the right motivation, and the proper lube, your discomfort will eventually ease. Before you engage in anal penetration, there are several measures you must take. The gluteus maximus also known as ass, azz, booty, buns, or cakes must be cleaned. Anal cleansing should be performed before sex and at times after as well by using over-the-counter disposable enemas from any local drugstore. If you run out of enemas, another cleaning tip is you can also use the old-fashioned rubber hot water bottle. Place lukewarm water with a cap full of hydrogen peroxide in the bottle as a solution. Caution: using cleaning products on a daily basis can cause damage to the anal lining or lead to dependence on the device.

The Gluteus Maximus a.k.a. The Booty
SS Rule 503

What sentence(s) in this rule stands out for you?

How would you define this rule for your social media followers?

Bootyology
SS Rule 503B

Just like there are names for the different types of penis, the booty or buttocks has its own labels and descriptions in the world of MAMs. Because the gluteus maximus in many cases is a prominent part of the male body, whether your role is top or bottom, more than likely, your posterior has a name. Some of the labels for booty are the curvy, regulation, fullback, and bathwater.

Curvy booty males can be slim, short, or tall, and yet his assets subtly stand out even under a tucked shirt. It's sexy, and some say it even looks eatable. His buns are so small you can grip them with both hands. A curvy booty belongs to that small-framed guy whose irresistibility is that he is comfortable being placed in almost any sexual bottom position.

Regulation booty means the posterior is height and weight proportionate; visually, it fits him perfectly. Regulation booty is unique because it has to do with individual acceptance of the ass that you find sexy. In other words, regulation booty doesn't have to stand out, but it has to be attractive to you.

Fullback booty is large, big, and bouncy. It is so big that it can't be hidden no matter what clothing is worn. Fullback booty could also describe a large-framed muscle man, or he could just be round and thick. If you're attracted to fullback booty, then for you mounting it is the end game.

Bathwater booty is the sexual ideal. He may not be handsome in the classic sense, but his body is so chiseled that his physique and posterior for you is perfection. The guy with a bathwater booty is so *phyne*, so emotionally attractive, and is so highly regarded that you will say or do anything to get into this select brand of cakes and cookies. The bottom line is if you are an ass man, then what type of cakes you are attracted to is an individual freedom that you have a right to exercise privately. The rules say have fun and remember to always enjoy the booty.

Bootyology
SS Rule 503B

What sentence(s) in this rule stands out for you?

How would you define this rule for your social media followers?

Analingus or Tossing Salad
SS Rule 504

The skill of analingus or rimming or ass eating or tossing salad is another highly developed art form perfected by MAMs. This sexual art form is achieved by using your tongue to passionately provide pleasure to the anus during foreplay. If you have the ideal in front of you, then the act of performing analingus will keep you erect, even without fellatio occurring. In other words, if you're eating the ass correctly, then you will be turned on without oral penis stimulation happening. This fetish has to do with the booty shape, the look, the smell, and the taste. Together, when these senses are stimulated, it motivates you to perform this act with perfection. On the receiving end, getting this type of head provides sensual pleasure. Many agree analingus feels good, and also, it is the ultimate anal relaxer.

In order to get your partner ready to discover the pleasures of rimming, start with having nonverbal conversations by using body language to convey your fetish or, as some would say, your freak. This act should be a part of foreplay; if you are a skilled top, then once again, you should start by orally discovering all of his erogenous zones. Anal finger manipulation while tossing salad is good advice. The fingers should gently roam the outer areas of his manhole while only going as deeply as he will allow. Once all his erogenous zones are stimulated, orally moving to his pelvis area is a good idea. This is when you guide him to either turn his buttocks toward you as you position him to go on fours. When this happens, the first thing to do is use your fingers to carefully open his cakes. At this point, in the process, if you've done your job, then his anus should be in your face!

Once that happens, your tongue should become a gentle yet firm wet arrow stimulating him with each level tasted and fingered. Some say true cake eating is sexual foreplay taken to another level for all involved. This fetish has little gray area; you either like eating cakes or you like your cakes eaten or you don't. Analingus is a popular form of sexual expression. Have a good time, but know the specifics. The rules draw your attention to the fact that despite its popularity, this fetish is considered risky behavior, and therefore, it is not safe sex. Just know what you're doing and who you're doing. Now choose!

Analingus or Tossing Salad
SS Rule 504

What sentence(s) in this rule stands out for you?

How would you define this rule for your social media followers?

Intercourse 101
SS Rule 505

Sex is not the sum total of who you are, but this activity plays a major role. In the male psyche, sex and intimacy can be one in the same; or on the other hand, they can mean two different things. According to the rules, male-to-male intercourse or the act of copulation or fucking has been described as the true physical intimacy. Physical intimacy in this case means to appreciate the natural feel of what only two males can do together. This natural sexual phenomenon cannot be taught in a classroom or even read in a book. It will only take place when you are alone with him, and there is sexual energy between the two of you. Once this happens, instinct will take over from there. When it comes to males, how sex happens really matters. The names given to the various sexual positions are vast and diverse. The rules invite you to take a look at four basic positions which can be achieved during intercourse. They are the HN position, the FD position, the FF position, and the TS position. Gone are heterosexual terms like doggy style or missionary because you are not a canine, and sex is not about saving souls!

Let's begin with the hands-and-knees position. The HN position occurs when you are so comfortable, so opened that you are ready to be penetrated while on your hands and knees. In other words, you are on all fours. When you are in the HN position, make sure the back is arched and the anus is exposed, so you can allow the pelvis to be held.

There are times in this position when you are mounted, while he uses his body and his penis enhancing access inside of you. The HN position can also occur when both of you are standing with your palms against the wall. There are benefits to standing or being on all fours while in the HN position. When he is inside you, he can gently bite the nape of your neck or pull your hair, or he can kiss your earlobes while simultaneously stroking your penis to the point of ejaculation. This is one of the most popular positions—if you are the one on top. If you are the one on the bottom, stamina is needed; keep in mind you are taking every inch of the penis while in the HN position.

The FD position is one of the first postures that MAMs discover even before the actual penetration. The FD position means face down, lying on your stomach. Sometimes called the discovery position, FD is learned as early as your sleepover days or in summer camp or add your story here. Most males learn early on about grinding or dry humping and how this act can turn into real penetration while in the FD position. When you have intercourse with another male, the act is an individual experience that's expressed within the sex itself. If done with passion, the FD position can be pure poetry.

The FF or face-to-face position happens when the mutual sexual attraction is so powerful that you are able to comfortably be on your back, with both legs in the air while being penetrated.

There are only two ways this sensual activity can occur comfortably, either with a pillow under the buttocks or upright facing him on edge of the bed or a counter or tabletop or another flat surface.

The FF is by far one of the most physically versatile of all the positions. Ultimately, both your eyes meet during this sexual encounter. FF is enjoyed because it allows for passionate kissing along with nipple play if you like. In this position, you can pull his legs back or spread them open or place them together up in the air. FF allows you to orally engage in foot worshiping, and on a few occasions, if the bottom's penis is large enough, you can give him head in this position as well. Riding the penis by sitting on it, is another variation of FF. Sometimes called riding dirty, sitting on top allows the bottom to control the rhythm of the strokes during the sexual encounter.

The last basic position discussed is called the TS, and it means being penetrated while on your side. When you are performing sex in the TS position, the one on top is in main control of the rhythm. The TS can be done while you hold his thigh and legs as you take your penis in and out, providing pleasure to his anus with each sexual thrust. This can also happen when the bottom brings his leg forward to his chest, prompting an erotic sensation to the penis while stimulating the anus at the same time. One variation on this position is when the top does what some call backward penetration. Backward penetration happens when the top turns around while sexing you facing the opposite way. Picture his face at your feet and your face is at his feet.

What position is your favorite?

How many of them do you know?

Which one is more comfortable for you?

How often have you started out in one of the positions and ended up going through all four?

Intercourse 101
SS Rule 505

What sentence(s) in this rule stands out for you?

How would you define this rule for your social media followers?

Definition of Top, Bottom, and Versatile
SS Rule 506

As anyone in the legacy and ikonoclass stages will tell you, terms used today to indentify same-sex roles were nonexistent prior to the late eighties. During those times, males got together purely on instinct in many cases using only May-dar. Prior to the end of the twentieth century, each had to figure out what role the other played just before the sex act occurred. As you can imagine the unknown made for an awkward situation once you were in the privacy of the bedroom. Back then, code words which were not understood by heterosexuals were created. In those days, MAMs even had to become more sophisticated about how to let others know sexual roles while in public. Some in the community used baseball terminology, earrings, and even handkerchiefs to send coded sexual messages to one another. For instance, if you wore an earring or handkerchief on one side, it meant you were passive; and if these items were worn on the other side, it meant you were aggressive. Prior to the term *bisexual,* males in this group were referred to as *men who played for both teams.* Toward the end of the twentieth century, MAMs were able to popularize three basic labels to identify sexual roles in relationships. The names are indentified by many today as either top, bottom, or versatile.

Before discussing the rules about sexual labels and roles, we must clear up the myth about the catch all term *versatile.* The rules theorize that the sexual term *versatile* is more of an ideal than a reality.

Anyone who's versatile, top, or bottom will tell you that he is comfortable with one sexual role more than another. In other words, he may be more of a natural top, but he will bottom or vice versa. It is human nature to prioritize your wants according to how you feel. With this in mind, the rules have identified a few of the labels that men attracted to the same sex take on during intimate encounters. There are about six main labels for both tops and bottoms according to the rules. In other words, there are three roles for a top to play and three roles for the bottoms. First up, let's start with a brief look at the top role descriptions.

MAMs who take on the top role during sex are identified as true total tops, versatile tops, and oral tops. If you are a true total top, then you can appreciate a good posterior when you see one. When you do secure it, there is an automatic inclination to explore the sexual conquest. Discovering his lips, feeling his hips, and finding the spot to hit are the trademarks of a true total top. This group uses dominant energy with expertise. In other words, true total tops know how to make him feel sexually opened and relaxed. There may be times a brief thought about bottoming creeps through your mind, but it's quickly dismissed. In the scheme of things, you could care less what he's doing with his penis while bottoming for you. A true total top earns his name for a reason. It's not that he won't touch a penis, but that's about as far as it goes. If you ask him for head or ask him to bottom, he will hurt your feelings! In a room with others, when it comes to the sex act, the true total top will more than likely be the dominant male in that situation.

Versatile tops are open to bottoming under mostly three conditions. These conditions include:

- When you have to keep a lover.
- The guy is so hot that bottoming is the only way you can have him.
- Every now and then you feel like being submissive.

It makes sense that this group's appreciation of how to treat a bottom comes from a deeper place than other tops. Most versatile tops know how to consistently create sexual passion. In other words, it means making sure to give the bottom the total array of your skills. The facts are that versatile tops are more sexually comfortable than any other top in this group. Masters in the bedroom, versatile tops are considered the "assologist" of the same sex world. The reputation comes from the time and effort you take in sensual anal pleasing. In many cases, your sexual skills are so precise and so accurate you are a favorite of all those with whom you are intimate. If you are a versatile top, then you are very selective about when to take on the bottom role. Many in this group believe that to give up your cakes to another male is a scared act not shared with just anyone. In many parts of the community, some even say versatile tops are the ideal dream if you are considering relationships. Magic is made when two versatile tops are engaged in a sexual encounter, each of you bottoming for one another.

In most cases, while the two of you may have fun, it almost never works out in the long term. After all, at the end of the day, both of you have the same sexual appetite; and one day, the other top will get tired being the bottom or vice versa.

If you are an oral top, then often your pleasure can be derived from either his penis or his cakes. An oral top's head game, as they say, is tight; this group usually does not discriminate whether it's fellatio or analingus—no problem. This type of top can toss a salad like a gourmet chef! The act of orally stimulating an ass or making love to his penis is enough to make you ejaculate even before you enter the anus. In the world of other tops, freak is your middle name, and you live up to that moniker! One of your preferences is the bottom with a WMD; it's big, it's large, and to you, that's excitement. Oral top techniques are the envy of the MAM world. The fellatio skills you possess are the stuff of fairy tales and folklore! There's not category that can come close to performing analingus like you can. Oral tops will know how to turn up the freak dial to please you, but remember just because he likes to perform oral gratification does not necessarily mean he wants penetration.

Definition of Top, Bottom, and Versatile
SS Rule 506

What sentence(s) in this rule stands out for you?

How would you define this rule for your social media followers?

Bottoms
SS Rule 506B

Men are attracted to the same sex who bottom are sometimes categorized into three distinct labels of their own. They are the real bottom, the power bottom, and the versatile bottom. The real bottom has a natural innate tendency to be penetrated. This group is highly skilled in the art of the fellatio and has provided many memories using them. tTops agree that the look, the shape, and even the taste of your buttocks are grade A+. If you are a real bottom, then having your penis pleasured during sex may not be a turn on for you. This group of bottoms is mostly into pleasing the top. Sexual satisfaction is derived from the chase and the conquest. For real bottoms, ejaculation for the most part happens after the sex is over, sometimes with help but usually alone. Some bottoms in this group, more times than not, have to be careful not to equate good sex with something more, no matter how well you thought you bottomed!

The power bottom is turned on by a penis that is above average in length and/or width. In other words, they prefer WMDs and LRMs. Anything smaller just won't do because for many of you, it is a size queen culture. What distinguishes a power bottom from others is the sexual arousal that happens by the anticipation of being penetrated. In other words, you have unconsciously trained yourself mentally and physically for dick endurance. As a power bottom, you are turned on by a large penis in your anus because it makes you erect, resulting in ejaculation which leads to nutting it out. Moreover, it is self-evident that you know how to get him up, get on it, and jerk yourself off while riding his large phallus. Some power bottoms can handle double penetration; which means having two penises inside of you at the same time.

Another quality is you can bottom for two or more men within a twenty-four-hour time frame. Like you, many power bottoms don't mind when tops play with your penis as his is already inside you. Falling in love is not really your goal; you are having sexual fun. While power bottoms are ready to take on large penises, biologically as the years go by, stamina for this activity can wan. It's important to note that this type of bottoming has a short lifespan lasting only for a few years at best. Therefore, the rules highly recommend regular medical checkups. Hemorrhoids, along with other more serious internal issues, can come up after being penetrated by large penis over a period of time for multiple times.

Last but not least, there is the versatile bottom. If you are in this group, just playing the submissive role in the bedroom will get very boring, very fast. While you are more comfortable bottoming, if the situation calls for it, you have no problem in the top role! The need to top occasionally is important; this skill will serve you well when you consider a long-term relationship. Of all the bottoms, you are more open-minded to testing the limits of male-to-male sexuality. The versatile bottom is the only category of bottom that has the skills to persuade or perhaps seduce another MAM to explore his freak or fetishes. This group has been known to make tops and other bottoms feel relaxed enough to explore outside of their own sexual comfort zones. The sensual rhythm you posses, along with your mattress performances, have caused down low tops to come out of the closet and bisexuals to ring your door bell in the middle of the night! In other words, versatile bottoms know the answer to the question about the 3:00 a.m. phone call!

The rules say if you are a bottom, be a good one, and make your name legendary in the minds of every top you encounter.

Bottoms
SS Rule 506B

What sentence(s) in this rule stands out for you?

How would you define this rule for your social media followers?

Frottage
SS Rule 507

Frottage or frot is the name given when males are sexually intimate with each other, without oral or anal penetration. Sometimes known as dry-humping or grinding, this sex act can happen when you're naked together or even while you're somewhat clothed. More than any other form of sex, frottage has to do with the coordination of your mind, body, and spirit. When you are engaging in this act, your mind must be free to concentrate onto the exploration of his body. It is inevitable that you will create a fantasy, thinking what it would be like if physical penetration actually happened with him. Frottage has a natural male physicality that heightens passion which can be fulfilling to both of you. There is a connection made when male bodies physically take each other to sensual levels without penetration. The sexual goal is to find each other's sweet spots. Frottage is foreplay to the next level!

If done correctly, both of you will achieve arousal without anal penetration. Spirit is achieved with this activity when both of you instinctively know that an attraction exist. It's evidenced through your honesty to discuss frottage as a choice in the first place. When there's spirit in frottage, your mind frees itself to enjoy the physical stimulation that is derived from this contact. Another aspect of spirit is the ability to see beauty beyond physical features, including body size or body shape. When the mind, the body, and the spirit are in sync, ejaculation will occur. Performing this act is one of the safest sex that males can engage in with each other.

Fellatio and the use of other tongue skills are permitted but not necessary during this sexual act. Arousal is enhanced while both your bodies are going up and down, passionately embracing one another to deliver the ultimate climax. There are some who believe full analingus is okay during frottage; the rules state this is a slippery slope, but it's up to you.

Many MAMs who engage in frottage may have a powerful fear of contracting HIV or other STDs. This fear prevents some from engaging in oral or anal penetration. Then there are others who may use frottage as a shield against going all the way with another man. Still there are several of you who believe in the notion that engaging in frottage means you're still heterosexual. Of course, that notion is flatly not true. Having said that, most who engage in this type of sex do it because you really like it!

One final point: the broader definition of frottage states that this act can also occur in public, fully clothed. Some may find it appealing to attempt frottage within a crowd, like at a parade or on a rush-hour subway trains or other public places. This type of behavior can mean criminal prosecution; make sure you have permission. Still don't know what frottage is? Just think about jacking off with someone else or even engaging in male wrestling, or think about two males riding the same bike!

Frottage
SS Rule 507

What sentence(s) in this rule stands out for you?

How would you define this rule for your social media followers?

Masturbation and More
SS Rule No. 507B

Like frottage, masturbation is another form of safe sex that many males enjoy. The fine art of ejaculation is discovered during the neophyte stage; that's when you begin to notice the hard on you can't control. Masturbation, or rubbing one out, or jerking off is the most frequent form of sex you have over a lifetime. For some, this type of sex can be more enjoyable than oral, anal, or even frottage activity. One unique feature of masturbation is that it can be performed privately or even with someone else. The term used when one or more are involved in the act is called mutual masturbation. Having said that it is the only real sexual act that doesn't require another person. In most cases, it does require a fantasy in your thoughts or a porno steaming on your screen! Masturbation is a perfectly healthy activity to release sexual tension. Some use lotions or other lubricants, and then again, you may not need anything. The rules say use what feels good to you.

Another form of safe sex that can be connected with masturbation is watching pornography. Since the beginning of the twentieth century, porn has moved from film to videos to DVDs to now on adult Web sites and even on your mobile device. Porn is a good way to help illustrate the definitions for voyeurism and exhibitionism. If you are turned on by being watched while performing sex, then chances are you're an exhibitionist. However, if you like watching sex acts performed without your participation, then maybe you're a voyeur. While both activities are centered around sex, only voyeurism is considered safe.

Another activity that feels good to the anus is using sex toys. There are many different types of toys used for pleasure. Find out what you are comfortable with. Here again, it's your choice. When it comes to these devices, the rules recommend only one toy for the anus, a dildo. Even with dildos, you still have to be careful with what you are doing. Remember, placing a foreign object inside your anus other than a tongue or a penis is prohibited because these objects can injure the lining inside your rectum.

Masturbation and More
SS Rule 507B

What sentence(s) in this rule stands out for you?

How would you define this rule for your social media followers?

Three-Ways, Orgies, and Sex Parties
SS Rule 508

It is the desire for many human beings to have an intimate connection with another person. Within most same-sex relationships, copulation is the ultimate goal. Copulation (fucking) means sex between two individuals, and it is one of the most acceptable forms of intimacy whether you are heterosexual or homosexual. This commonality with heterosexuals means some of you desire relationship fulfillment one at a time. Then again, there are many others who will likely have sex outside of the relationship. This phenomenon has to do with an internal physical drive that can cause some males to struggle with a commitment to just one person sexually. When sex becomes routine or is somehow stressed, you will find yourself giving into this internal physical drive. At this point, you seek out alternate forms of sexual engagement. Ultimately, these forms of sexual engagements, if not addressed, can happen outside your relationship.

When this occurs, there are two choices you think about. Some may give in to these desires without your partner's knowledge. On the other hand, if the two of you have an understanding, then he may join you. With this in mind, the rules invite you to briefly take a look at three forms of sexual engagements outside of traditional copulation. Identified as threesomes, orgies, and sex parties, they are as old as mankind. If these engagements are done as an option and not because of a habit, then the experience can create lifelong memories.

The three-way or threesome obviously occurs when all of you engaged in sensual sexual activity with each other at the same time. The first thing to remember is that when engaging in a threesome, there will be two of you who are more attracted to each other than you are to the third male. There are many reasons for this occurrence; one is maybe the threesome was organized by a couple, and you are outside of that unit. Another general reason could be that two of the three strangers may have a better sexual vibe than the other one. When this happens in threesomes, it does not mean you can't enjoy the experience. Just know what you're getting into. As long as all are involved in the decision, what you do depends on the rules established with the other two. The ideal threesome includes a combination of at least a versatile top or one versatile bottom in the mix. The third man can play any sexual role if the other two are included.

Be warned: without one of these ingredients, chances are the three-way will not be enjoyed by all parties. Threesomes can also occur in other combinations, like with maybe two true total tops and one power bottom or the other way around.

There are names attached to some of the sexual positions accomplished during threesomes, for example, the sex roast, the double penetration, and the silver chain. The sex roast, also known in the pejorative as a pig roast, happens when you are orally satisfying one penis while another penis is in your anus at the same time. Double penetration describes the sex act where two penises are inside of your anus at the same time during the face-to-face position. The silver chain means that all three of you are engaged in simultaneous fellatio. In other words, all three of you are sucking dick at the same time!

Orgy or group sex occurs when there are more than three engaged in sexual activity with the intent purpose of being with multiple partners during the act. An authentic orgy in most cases is an agreed-upon, planned event by invitation. There is no requirement that you intimately know all the participants before the orgy begins. But if you partake in an orgy, then usually there should be a prior sexual connection between one or some of the other participants. This kind of sex starts with either two men disrobing and setting things off by first engaging in foreplay or straight to oral sex. When this occurs, the other participants will be able to let go of all their inhibitions so that a good time can be had by all. Orgies allow you and other participants to explore differences within the sexual encounter. Once this happens, you begin to concentrate on total erotic fulfillment. In an orgy, some say it is assumed that you will have sex with more than one person during the act.

Since the 1990s, a new phenomenon presented itself as a choice for MAMs to sexually engage with other like-minded individuals. A sex party is a semi-private event where you and others may pay a fee to gather in a space for the purpose of indiscriminate sex anonymously. Unlike an orgy, in a sex party, you can choose to concentrate on one person, or you can have multiple partners. This form of group sex is a money-making venture for the host and allows other MAMs a means of physical escape without revealing names.

This anonymity enhances the experiences that you have when engaging in sex parties. These parties, if done properly, start with an invitation list of other MAMs on your social media or e-mail . The advertisement contains the date, the time, and the place of the event. Included with the price of admission are the rules of the party, like what's allowed and not allowed. When you enter the party, be prepared to take off your street clothes, placing them in a black bag as you strip down to either your underwear or a towel. If towels are there, then at some parties they are deliberately small enough that, if you are a top, your ass is covered; and if you are feeling like a bottom, then the towel covers your penis. At some sex parties, liquor, along with 420 weed, is permissible. Lighting is kept low, allowing you to use your hands to feel your way around the room until your eyes adjust to the semidarkness. There are some parties that will have pornography on the screen, along with a sex sling hanging from the ceiling. Sex parties are one of the only forms of sexual activity that incorporate copulation and threesomes and orgies at one event.

Three-Ways, Orgies, and Sex Parties
SS Rule 508

What sentence(s) in this rule stands out for you?

How would you define this rule for your social media followers?

S&M, Raw Sex, and Breeding
SS Rule 509

Sadomasochism is a highly developed sexual art form that has its own rules concerning sensation, trust, and limit setting. The term *sadomasochism,* or S&M to the civilian's ear, congers up the forbidden. The thought of performing S&M for some means out of the mainstream, intimidation, scary, and even painful sex. As a matter of fact, many of you are not even sure if sadomasochism falls under the definition of a sexual act. On the other hand, there are those who view S&M as a normalizing experience. The sadomasochist believes pain and pleasure are the epitome of sexual liberation; also, it is the highest form of carnal expression.

By the way, sadomasochism was recorded in human history as early as the tenth century. However, this specialized sexual act got its name from the actions of two Frenchmen. During the late 1800s, the Marquis de Sade published manuscripts endorsing the notion that inflicting pain was the height of sexual achievement. Around the same time, Leopold von Sacher-Masoch was known to engage in the sexually submissive role. He also participated in and wrote about the pleasures of being spanked.

S&M can take place with two or more people; it begins with establishing rules about who plays the role of master and slave. In other words, who will be the sadist (master) and who will be the masochist (slave). Before any activity takes place, one of the most important aspects about sadomasochism is trust.

It is imperative that you establish trust with one another before embarking in S&M. When you engage in this kind of sexual activity, it makes sense to know each other's limits. It is a good idea to create a safe word if you have reached your limit while engaging in this activity. Once you've establish your own rules, then it's time to choose your fantasy. The limits are up to you; it can include terms like *submission, coercion,* and *domination.* The use of restraints can be a part of it as well. Items worn during S&M can include leather, chains, chaps, jock straps, and cock rings. There are other options worn like police, fire, biker, and military uniforms. When engaging in S&M, what you wear can be infinite! This fetish is about sexual pleasure and pain in order to achieve ejaculation. No wonder some of the crucial elements of this activity are spanking, slapping, and biting, just to name a few. Bondage, rough nipple, and anal play are all aspects of the S&M sexual extremes.

Several decades ago, this form of sexual expression was considered a fringe sexual activity. Today, it is no longer an extreme counterculture secret. If done correctly between consenting adults, S&M can be a pleasurable experience. For those in the community who may judge this activity in a negative way, here are some questions you should ponder:

> *Have I, or anyone I've been with, verbally given instructions during sex? Have I, or anyone I've been with, played a little "slap and tickle" game during sex?*
>
> *Have I, or anyone I've been with, pinched or bitten nipples during sex?*

If you answered yes to any of these three questions, then you have already engaged in a form of S&M!

S&M, Raw Sex, and Breeding
SS Rule 509

What sentence(s) in this rule stands out for you?

How would you define this rule for your social media followers?

Raw Sex and Breeding
SS Rule 509B

Mankind has been perfecting the condom for more than four hundred years. But it was the advent of the HIV/AIDs epidemic that made latex condoms the leading contraceptive used today. The reason this contraceptive became so popular was because males who are attracted to the same sex, like millions of others at that time, were dying from AIDS. In the 1980s, funding, treatments, and medications enjoyed today did not exist. Fear griped the community; MAM's awareness about using protection became a matter of life and death.

However, over the past few years, especially within some of the neophyte, ingénue, and supernova age ranges, raw sex has staged a comeback. The generations born during and after the AIDs crisis may psychologically feel invincible to sexually transmitted diseases. The belief that somehow you are immune fuels this risk-taking sexual behavior.

Raw sex or bareback, for MAMs, means having anal intercourse without condoms. Breeding or seeding happens when while having raw sex, you ejaculate inside the anus. The very concept of breeding comes out of the idea that you want to give him what you have by sexually transmitting it from your penis through his anus. If you engage in sex without a condom, your actions state that the risk outweighs the stimulating sensation felt in the skin to skin sexual experience. If you visit any adult Web site that features same-sex male intercourse, you will discover that bareback and breeding movies are extremely popular. The rules remind you that both raw sex and breeding are called risky behaviors for a reason; stay informed, get regular medical checkups, and be aware of the chances you are taking. If you are positive and knowingly spread HIV, then this action could be seen as a crime.

Raw Sex and Breeding
SS Rule 509B

What sentence(s) in this rule stands out for you?

How would you define this rule for your social media followers?

Sexually Transmitted Diseases (STDs)
SS Rule 510

The Center for Disease Control (CDC) reporting on the 2009 study of STDs reveals: *In total, the CDC estimates that there are approximately 19 million new STD infections each year, which costs the U.S. healthcare system 16 billion dollars annually. It costs individuals even more in terms of acute and long-term health care consequences. Since 2000, the largest increase in syphilis cases has been among men who have sex with men (MSM). In 2009, MSM accounted for nearly two-thirds of syphilis cases (62%), up from just 4% in 2000 (Center for Disease Control, Trends in Sexually Transmitted Diseases in the USA, 2009).*

This CDC report leaves you to wonder: does the spike in STDs have direct correlation with the popularity of bareback sex and breeding within the MAM community? Sexually transmitted diseases or STDs have been affecting mankind for as long as there has been civilized society. The legacy generation will recall when STD is simply known as a social disease. The ikonoclass may recall when it evolved into the catchall term *venereal disease* or just VD. Many agree the only major sexually transmitted disease recently discovered in the later part of the twentieth century was HIV/AIDS. According to medical facts, STD is classified either as a disease that affects the genitals or it's a viral infection. The rules will explain two of the diseases that affect the genitals like syphilis and gonorrhea. Also covered are three of the viral diseases like herpes, hepatitis, and of course, HIV.

Sexually Transmitted Diseases (STDs)
SS Rule 510

What sentence(s) in this rule stands out for you?

How would you define this rule for your social media followers?

Syphilis
SS Rule510B

One disease on the rise in the MAM community is syphilis, which can affect both your penis and anus. There are four stages of syphilis: primary, secondary, latent, and tertiary. The primary stage is triggered when you have unprotected sex with a person who is already infected. In this stage, syphilis looks like a firm red sore or a noticeable break in the skin. The medical community calls this sore a chancre. This sore is painless; it can appear on the penis, anus, and even the mouth. In other words, it shows up where the syphilis entered the body.

If this chancre is not treated within about thirty days, then it may disappear; that is when the secondary stage appears. At this point, the chancre is gone, replaced by growing rashes to several parts of your body. Along with the rashes, you may also experience fever and swollen glands. There are other physical changes in your body during the secondary stage like weight loss and hair loss, to name a few.

The latent stage, along with the tertiary stage, occurs when both the primary and secondary conditions have disappeared. These stages can last for more than ten years. When latent and tertiary syphilis is diagnosed, you lack muscle control. Also, there may be some paralysis, blindness, and other issues that affect the brain. The bottom line is if syphilis is left untreated, this disease can cause death!

Syphilis can be treated by what's called intramuscular injections. The effective treatment for this disease is an antibiotic medication called penicillin. Other antibiotics can be substituted if you are allergic. Get tested because if you are treated within the first three months of contracting the disease, then your chances for recovery is assured.

Syphilis
SS Rule510B

What sentence(s) in this rule stands out for you?

How would you define this rule for your social media followers?

Gonorrhea a.k.a. the Claps
SS Rule 510C

The other bacterial disease that MAMs should look out for is gonorrhea, also known as the claps. Like syphilis, gonorrhea locates itself in your penis or mouth or anus. The difference is that gonorrhea infects the inside of the urine canal otherwise known as the urethra. In some men, not only is the infection painful when peeing, but urine may come out as a thick pus-like substance. Symptoms can appear at around one to ten days after you contract it from having sex with an infected person. This disease mostly affects MAMs who are in the late neophyte and in the early ingénue stages more than any other generation of MAM maturity.

If you find yourself experiencing these symptoms, then get tested. The treatment for this illness is the use of several antibiotics given in the form of at least two treatments. There are many more facts surrounding this disease. The rules encourage you to seek as much information as you can through your local health department.

Gonorrhea a.k.a. the Claps
SS Rule510C

What sentence(s) in this rule stands out for you?

How would you define this rule for your social media followers?

Hepatitis A
SS Rule 510D

Hepatitis is a viral disease, which means it affects the blood and internal organs in the body. The diagnosis of hepatitis indicates that your liver is inflamed because of exposure to this disease. According to the CDC, there are five types of this disease: hepatitis A, B, C, D, and E. The rules require you to investigate each alphabet so that you can understand for yourself how they are contracted. If you perform analingus, you should make sure that you are eating a clean booty, for it is one of ways this disease is contracted. There is a chance that even if he appears clean, it may not prevent you from contracting hepatitis. Ingesting fecal matter is an activity where hepatitis A is contracted. The facts are that even alcohol addiction can also trigger this disease. The signs of hepatitis starts with flu-like symptoms, including feeling tired, and even rashes may break out. When you urinate, the color is dark brown, and your feces are a very light color. In addition, hepatitis have been known to turn your skin and eyes yellow; the sense of taste is distorted as well.

    The good thing about hepatitis A is, when treated, it does not lead to a chronic infection, but the other types of this disease can. Treatment for hepatitis A can take up to six months. Keep in mind that each case, along with each intervention can be different depending on the individual. The point is, when it comes to hepatitis treatment, follow the instructions of your physician. There is a vaccine for children beginning at age one and for people who don't have the disease traveling outside of the USA.

Hepatitis A
SS Rule 510D

What sentence(s) in this rule stands out for you?

How would you define this rule for your social media followers?

Herpes
SS Rule 510E

Herpes could be another disease that you should look out for if you are sexually active. Viral herpes and cold sores fall into the same infection category; except with herpes, there are some differences. The disease you should concern yourself with is called genital herpes. This type of herpes can appear as a sore in your mouth or on your penis or in your anus. The sore disappears and reappears every few weeks within a year; genital herpes can be painful when it appears. Also, when the sore is present and you have sexual contact with the infected person, you are at risk of exposing yourself to the disease. If you have herpes, safe sex should be practiced even when the sore is not visible. As of this printing, there is no cure for this disease, but treatment with antiviral medications helps contain its outbreak.

Herpes
SS Rule 510E

What sentence(s) in this rule stands out for you?

How would you define this rule for your social media followers?

HIV
SS Rule510F

A CDC study found that, one in five or 19% MSM in 21 major cities were infected with HIV, and nearly half (44%) were unaware of their infection. In this study, 28% of black MSM were HIV-infected, compared to 18% of Hispanic/Latino MSM and 16% of white MSM. Other racial/ethnic groups of MSM also have high numbers of HIV infections, including American Indian/Alaska Native MSM (20%) and Native Hawaiian/Pacific Islander MSM (18%) [HIV among Gay Bisexual and Other Men Who Have Sex with Men (MSM), CDC 2011].

HIV remains on the rise within the same-sex male population for more than thirty plus years after the first case was diagnosed.

HIV means you have a human immunodeficiency virus. HIV is diagnosed when the infection has lowered your T-cells to a few hundred and the viral load in your body is over a thousand. HIV attaches themselves onto your healthy cells, making them ineffective when a virus enters your body.

When this occurs, blood test reveals a high viral load count. If you have HIV, your body is open to several illnesses because this disease compromises your immune system. Many common illnesses include upper respiratory issues, weight loss, lymphoid, and other swollen glands. If left untreated with cocktail of medications or you reinfect yourself by engaging in unprotected sex, then it's almost assured that HIV can turn into AIDS. By the time you are diagnosed with AIDS, there are life or death decisions for you to make.

The bottom line is to be honest with yourself concerning your own HIV status. Being honest with yourself is easier said than done; getting comfortable with this health issue will take time after first learning about your status. The rules state the only way you will free yourself from this burden is to discuss your with diagnosis with someone else. But before anything happens, get tested, get diagnosed, and take the prescribed course of medication. The thing to do is to get connected to a medical professional or a health clinic or an HIV social service program. This connection is paramount in keeping this disease from spreading and becoming a killer. Today, there are a number of effective HIV medications available; and if taken as prescribed, chances are you will live a full, healthy, and abundant life. Some believe that homophobia and other cultural stigmas prevent some MAMs from getting tested. The rules point out that if you live in a small town or in a large city, the test for HIV is guaranteed by federal law to be totally confidential. Learn more about HIV; there is so much information just waiting. Keep in mind: this kind of research can save your life.

HIV
SS Rule 510F

What sentence(s) in this rule stands out for you?

How would you define this rule for your social media followers?

The Rules on History and the Bible, the Torah, and the Quran

HBTQ Rules 100–110

Same-sex attraction has been a part of the human experience since the evolution of mankind. Society debated same-sex attraction since before the idea of one God existed. The Greek philosopher Aristotle was one of the first thinkers to hypothesize about male anal stimulation. But it wasn't until Christianity became the dominant religion in Europe more than two thousand years ago that MAMs were labeled as outcasts of society. Whether or not you believe in the Bible or the Torah or the Quran, understand that fear, prejudice, and cultural bias toward same-sex attraction stems from these three books. Today, there remain federal and state laws concerning same-sex relationships, especially when marriage and/or copulation are involved. These laws have enabled society to deem MAM relationships as somehow evil, un-natural, even using the term *abomination* to describe what they believe God commands. Because of those messages, many churchgoing men who are attracted to the same sex, at one time or another, questioned:

Was I born this way?
Why do I have these feelings for other males?
Why am I so ashamed to reveal my true self?
Am I really an abomination like the pastor said?

Questions like these have complicated answers; the HBTQ rules will help you build a personal blueprint so that you can frame the answers for yourself. Although the evidence continues to evolve, it is clear that environment has nothing to do with your same-sex birthright.

The goal of this chapter is to provide information about your natural place in history and how men who are attracted to the same sex are documented throughout the Torah, the Quran, even the Bible in both the Old and New Testament. The historic significance of same-sex attraction, along with genetics and your relationship to all life, is explained. What is the real message behind the story of Sodom and Gomorrah? The laws defined within Leviticus are clarified as well. Stories of male relationships, such as Jonathan and David, are also explored. The Apostle Paul's epistles or letters to Timothy, Romans, and the Corinthians are presented and analyzed. In addition, these rules were written primarily to educate many religious supporters who are attracted to the same sex who at times may experience abuse during Sunday sermons. Finally, the HBTQ rules invite you to the Book of Matthew where some argue the real meaning of the Bible is contained. For example, many say to see this spiritual truth in action, check out any Unity Fellowship Church Movement or similar liberation theology-based churches across the country. Here are the HBTQ rules, beginning from 100 to 110.]

Nature's Scheme
HBTQ Rule 101

In nature's scheme, you are not alone just because you are a male attracted to the same sex. The rules are clear: your nature is not a lifestyle choice. It is a different life, which is just as valuable as a heterosexuals'. There are times when others have judged your right to be who you were born to be. This kind of message indicates that at the "table of mankind", there is no space available because of your natural behavior. As a MAM, internalize that the table of equality is huge and all-encompassing. Therefore, it is assured that not one part of the human race can be seated at the table until males who are attracted to the same sex are seated there as well.

The debate concerning MAMs in today's society asks the question: is your internal makeup for same-sex attraction natural, or was it influenced by your physical environment? There have been arguments about this question since the early twentieth century. Well-documented theories have been presented and debunked, and the debate continues.

While progress has been made about nature versus nurture, confusion over same-sex attraction remains. There are those who have created unproven theories such as all men are born bisexual. This theory goes on to state that during early life, males evolve either heterosexual or homosexual. Some still believe the myth that same-sex attraction occurs when there is not a father in the home.

Then there are those who think that the mother overprotected the son and she did not allow him to socialize as most male children do. Another popular notion is that the parents did not force the male child to find an interest in sports.

There are some who even assume that an unfortunate circumstance may be the cause of same-sex attraction, for example, he was raped or molested as a child, or he was "turned out" in prison . . . that's why he's like that. The rules state that there are many heterosexual men in this world who did not grow up with a father, and many heterosexual men were raised by overprotective mothers—just ask their wives or girlfriends.

Moreover, rape and molestations are traumatic and violent acts that have nothing to do with same-sex attraction. There are studies published that prove how counterintuitive these myths are to your gender identity. In nature, there are no mistakes, just like the changes in the seasons or like the moon's influence over the ocean tides. As a MAM, sex attraction is your natural birthright—you had no choice in the matter.

Nature's Scheme
HBTQ Rule 101

What sentence(s) in this rule stands out for you?

How would you define this rule for your social media followers?

On Genetics
HBTQ Rule 102

It was genetically preordained from the time you were in your mother's womb that it was your blessing in life to be attracted to the same sex. Think about it: ever since you were a small child, there was something about the male gender that brought you either great pleasure, comfort, and fascination. As a far back as preadolescence, some of you more than likely had a strange feeling for your first best friend. How you secretly loved that famous male personality who flashed upon the screen. What about the guys in the neighborhood you admired and dared to ask yourself why you were attracted to these males?

Well, it all has to do with your genetic and biological makeup. This fact compels some of you to ask the question: why should I allow others to question my right to be my own innate self? Men who love the same gender have very stressful lives, living in a culture that is predominately heterosexual. The point is, this notion about who you are is a lifestyle choice and cannot be supported in a factual way.

There is evidence-based research that suggests genetics, along with womb environment and hormonal factors, may influence same-sex attraction. Some empirical researches suggest that the mother's womb environment play a key role in the genetic makeup of males. As an example, let's look at twin experiment a few years ago. The study found that genetically, there were groups where both sets of twins were attracted to the same sex, and then other studies found that only one twin became homosexual, while the other did not.

Another study published suggests that the pregnant mother being stimulated by the father's penis, along with womb birth order, can play a role in the same-sex attraction of a male child. There are epigenetic studies that found out women who have one of their two X chromosomes shut off while carrying an embryo are more likely to have a homosexual son.

Birth order research suggests that the younger the male son is to other male siblings, the more likely he will be attracted to the same sex. Research has discovered other commonalties, including more MAMs are left-handed, and the hair is more likely to grow in a counterclockwise fashion from the back of the skull. In other words, even with all of this evidence, the jury is still out about the "how" in genetics. .

Therefore, the rules tell you that the knowledge found in these studies means there's a realization that you may choose how to express yourself; however, you cannot choose who you were born to become internally. A male who is attracted to the same sex is not a choice someone would consider in a society that celebrates opposite-gender attraction.

On Genetics
HBTQ Rule 102

What sentence(s) in this rule stands out for you?

How would you define this rule for your social media followers?

Mankind and the Circle of Life
HBTQ Rule 103

Mankind is not the only species where same-sex attraction exists. In the animal kingdom, several hundred of species engage in this behavior. In most cases, they use this attraction as a form of greetings, or they use it to defuse hostilities. Studies have shown that this behavior is also practiced so that animals can gain an ally against other males. There are some mammals that use same-sex relations to form hunting teams so that they can increase the likelihood of catching prey.

In the animal kingdom, there are more than just sexual benefits in same-gender relationships. Take the male flour beetle; they have sex with other males to get rid of old sperm that is less effective for making baby beetles. One of the water mammals, male dolphins, engages in same-gender sex with each other to practice how to have sex with females. Male penguins and male flamingos have been studied building nests together and adopting foster chicks within their communities. Some male ostriches will openly court each other exclusively.

Finally, there is an animal that is closely related to human beings called the bonobo ape of Africa. The male bonobo's sexual appetite is so enormous that they spend most of their free time copulating, not with other females but with other males of their species. These apes are known as the true bisexuals of the animal kingdom!

Within the group of highly evolved primates, mankind or the human race, same-sex attraction is much more complicated. Homosexuality has been around since the dawn of mankind, and it has been well recorded throughout all the world's cultures. In the times before Christ, this type of pairing was viewed very differently than it is today.

In ancient Greece and Rome, men engaged in same-sex attraction openly and in high numbers. It was quite common for men to marry women but to also openly have male lovers at the same time. Ancient people did not use the terms we use today to describe male-to-male relationships. But same-sex attraction was very well documented, as well as celebrated. The evidence exists not only in worldwide historical documents but also in the arts, in theaters, and in other ancient cultural activities. Among scholars, it is well known that same-sex relations in pre-Christian times were considered innocuous, nonthreatening, or just another form of emotional expression.

Respected research in field explains that in many ancient African tribes, same sex behavior was expected and was a part of the male rite of passage. Sexual eroticism, such as mutual masturbation and anal sex, was included in the process. These practices were considered useful in order to ready the male for marriage to a female. In all the major ancient societies and cultures, male pairing prior to marriage was not looked upon as something done against nature but was very much a part of the fabric of life.

Erotic stimulation by having same sex experiences helped men gain knowledge and social interaction.

As a MAM, you owe it to yourself to take time out to research not only the history of mankind's same-sex attraction but how it all relates to the entire world culture. When you internalize that your existence matters, that knowledge will help you understand that you are not alone. As a part of the universal order, you are significant—your life is a part of a circle with actions and reactions. You will discover that same-sex attraction is not some sort of manufactured lifestyle fad like the religious right would have you believe. The rules will remind you, no matter what some might say, you are not a freak of nature—you are what nature designed!

Mankind and the Circle of Life
HBTQ Rule 103

What sentence(s) in this rule stands out for you?

How would you define this rule for your social media followers?

Jonathan and David
or
Love Stories
HBTQ Rule 104

The religious right will tell you that there are no same-sex relations written in the Bible. There are in fact at least three occurrences within the Bible where same-sex attraction is suggested. These occurrences are identified in the story of Ruth and Naomi and the friendship of Daniel and Ashpenaz. This rule explores the relationship between David and Jonathan, called one of the greatest love stories of all time. If you are a member of a religious right, then the chances of you hearing this interpretation of these stories are remote.

One reason for this is that many conservative churches are using highly edited Bibles like the Revised Standard Version (RSV) and other biblical books published in the twentieth century. These Bibles have at times distorted the messages in the King James Version (KJV). These distortions are purposeful and make it easy so that their ideas of intolerance can be promulgated. The religious right has so much power over the idea of homosexuality that even today the story of the four men and two women has never been given pop culture treatment. There are no plays, songs, or movie scripts about these biblical relationships. There is one consolation, a classic scripture repeated in quite a few wedding ceremonies that comes from the relationship between Ruth and Naomi.

In the Book of Ruth, she declared:

> *Where you go I go, and where you stay I will stay. Your people will be my people and your God my God. Where you die I will die, and there I will be buried. May the Lord deal with me, be it ever so severely, if anything but death separates you and me* (The Book of Ruth 1:16–17, the New International Version).

All you have to do is ask, what motivated Ruth to say those words? Was it passion, desire, or friendship? Or was it all three? Was their relationship closer than sisterly love?

In the Book of Daniel, you find him in a situation where he has to do what the king commanded of him. It was the duty of all eunuchs in the palace. The king wanted Daniel to have a drink with him. When Daniel decided not to accept the kings' hospitality, he found he needed the help of a special friend.

> *Now God had brought Daniel into favor and tender love with the prince of the eunuchs* (Daniel 1:9, KJV).

Was the great hero of the lions' den and witnessed to the fiery furnace involved with a man in a way that went beyond platonic friendship?

What is the backstory of Daniel's relationship to the prince of eunuchs?

What did "tender love" look like between two men during that time?

Why are there no references about Daniel and females within the book?

David, one the most famous kings of Israel, hero in the fight against the Philistines, the slayer of Goliath, and the son-in-law of Saul, had this experience:

> *And it came to pass, when he had made an end of speaking with Saul, that the soul of Jonathan was knit with the soul of David, and Jonathan loved him as his own soul. Then Jonathan and David made a convent, because he loved him as his own soul.*
>
> *And Jonathan stripped himself of the robe that was upon him, and gave it to David, and his garments, even to his sword, and his bow and his girdle* (1 Samuel 18:1, 3, 4, KJV).

As you investigate these verses closely, more questions arise: Did Saul allow David into the palace because he was a famous hero or because David and his son Jonathan were in love?

What does the term *knit* mean? Did it mean to be one with another?

What kind of convent did David and Jonathan have? Was it a marriage or was it just a friendship contract?

Did Jonathan take off all of his clothes to give to David for agape or brotherly love?

Did Jonathan take off all his clothes as an act of romantic love for David?

Reading further in 1 Samuel, you find that David was accepted in the king's palace, and as was the custom, the king gives David one of his daughters, who was Jonathan's sister to marry. On this occasion, Saul says to David:

> *Thou shall this day be my son-in-law, one in the twain* (1 Samuel 18:21, KJV).

In other words, Saul tells David that he now has the second opportunity to become his son-in-law. Why did King Saul make this statement about a second opportunity? David had not married any of the king's other daughters prior to this wedding.

Later in the story, Saul was angry with David about military leadership tactics, and the king was also jealous of his celebrity. Jonathan promised to intercede on David's behalf. Jonathan's only condition was that they make another commitment to each other:

> *And Jonathan caused David to swear again, because he loved him: for he loved him as he loved his own soul* (1 Samuel 20:17, KJV).

When there was no more hope, and as much as Jonathan tried, he was rebuffed by his father King Saul. David and Jonathan agreed to meet three days later whether the news was positive or negative. Here's what happened:

> *David arose out of a place from the south, and fell on his face to the ground, and bowed himself three times: and they kissed one another, and wept one with another, until David exceeded* (1 Samuel 20:41, KJV).

Now this passage is the most troubling to the religious community because no matter what version of the Bible you read, almost all of them agree that David and Jonathan kissed each other.

On the rare occasion, when discussed in a sermon, conservative churches use the reading from the Living Bible interpretation: *"And they sadly shook hands, tears running down their cheeks until David could weep no more."* It seems that the very idea a spiritual leader like David could ever perform a homosexual act like kissing another man is too much for the religious right to absorb. That was tame compared to "David exceeded"; now that's a powerful phrase. What does it mean to today's audience?

Why is this phrase so threatening to conservatives and so abhorrent that in many cases it is left out of Sunday sermons?

Does this phrase mean David becomes hard in an erotic way and therefore he had an erection?

Does this phrase mean David could cry no more until he calmed down?

The love story concludes when David, referring to Jonathan, laments, *Thy love to me was wonderful, surpassing the love of women* (2 Samuel 1:26, KJV). Is there a love between two men that can surpass the love that a woman can offer? Well, it is clear that David thought so and said it publicly just before he was named King of Judah.

Jonathan and David
or
Love Stories
HBTQ Rule 104

What sentence(s) in this rule stands out for you?

How would you define this rule for your social media followers?

Prehistory and Other Cultures
HBTQ Rule 105

Since the sixteenth century, fanatic groups like the religious right basically use at least five biblical books in an attempt to win what some believe to be an artificial argument about MAMs. This is the argument that says same-sex attraction, or your genetic makeup, is somehow against God. Before we take a look at those passages in the Bible, when attacked by the religious right, it is important to understand what the rules tell you about the Bible.

While the Bible is one of the greatest books of all time, what is included was literally edited and selected by the pagan Roman emperor named Constantine, around AD 325. Emperor Constantine, not a stupid man, took a look at the political climate of the day. During that time, the Roman Empire was losing its grip on Europe, primarily because of a new religion called Christianity. In order to preserve the Roman Empire, he made Christianity the official religion.

In addition, Constantine organized several religious leaders to convene and ordered them to agree to one book written in the language of that day—Greek and Latin—to provide religious guidelines to early Christians. The chapters or books of the Bible which combine many stories originally found in the Torah fall under basically seven categories. They are the historical books, the wisdom books, the prophetical books, the four gospels, the Acts of the Apostles, the letters of Paul and other writers, and the Book of Revelation.

In the sixth century, another holy book acknowledged by Muslims was created; this book is called the Quran. Muslims believe the Quran is a book of divine guidance and direction for all humanity. The text is considered words that they believe come directly from God. The Quran was revealed to Muhammad through the angel Gabriel over a period of twenty-three years. Muslims believe the Quran, with its 114 chapters, is God's final revelation to mankind. The Islamic view of same-sex relationships is that it is a sin.

In the Quran, there are references to what is referred to as the men of Lot or Lut. He is the same man that the Bible refers to in the story of Sodom and Gomorrah. Basically, the Quran says that if there are people who are attracted to the same sex among you, then you must cast them out because they are unclean. However—and here is the conflict—after they have been cast out, they may return once they have cleansed themselves. Some argue that Muhammad said if a man who is attracted to the same sex does not act on his desires and remains celibate, then he has not violated God's laws. In this context, it is important to understand that being celibate does not mean that you cannot masturbate. As a matter of fact, while this act is considered unclean, the only requirement for forgiveness is to shower or take a bath before the next prayer service. If this logic is followed by Muslims who are attracted to the same sex, then mutual masturbation with others is allowed so long as penetration does not occur. It's important to note that currently, there are about five official Muslim nations where same-sex intercourse carries the death penalty, including Saudi Arabia and Iran.

As you can see, the Islamic belief about homosexuality is complicated and controversial. History teaches you that if you explore what happened at the beginning of an idea, like finding out about the top three religious books in the United States, with this insight, you can arm yourself with information about how these books were created and what was their original intent. This knowledge should empower you to learn more about Christianity, Judaism, and Islam.

Prehistory and Other Cultures
HBTQ Rule 105

What sentence(s) in this rule stands out for you?

How would you define this rule for your social media followers?

Christianity: The Beginnings
HBTQ Rule 106

The rules state that for non ordained MAMs or a lay person, the key to biblical interpretation is understanding the words for yourselves and placing those words into a historical and cultural context. Once you've done so, use the information gained to apply to your own circumstances.

If you believe in the Bible, then you must recognize that this famous manuscript is a living and breathing document. Many agree that you can use the biblical book to intellectually fight the challenges that may arise in today's society.

As you learned in a previous HBQT rule, an idol worshiper ordered the making of the Bible and installed Christianity as the official religion of the Roman Empire. It was the crumbling Roman Empire that created Vatican City and established the first pope. Until the late fifteenth century, the pope controlled all religious thoughts and views in Europe's Middle Ages. It wasn't until Martin Luther caused a split in the Catholic Church that the pope's hold on Europe was released. At around the same time, there was a man who not only cheated on his wives, but he also killed several of them as well. Although he had his own issues, he made it possible for the Bible to be read in English. King Henry VIII in the fourteenth century changed the Bible from Latin to English so that it could be read to the public by priests and the pastors. There was not a king more brutal than King Henry VIII. His life has two positive legacies: translating the Bible into old English and being the father of Queen Elizabeth I, one of the MAMs' iconic figures.

After Queen Elizabeth I's reign, a MAM named King James I was inspired to have the Bible written into the words you read each Sunday; his book is a best seller even today. It has been documented that King James I was a bisexual man with sexual appetites that surpassed his cousin Queen Elizabeth I. While he had a wife, he was known to feature men in his court as well as in his bedroom chambers. These are historical facts of how imperfect men played an important role in the book called the Bible. If the god you believe in gave man the Bible and divine grace allowed these men to complete God's work, then it makes logical sense the same God can do great things for you!

Christianity: The Beginnings
HBTQ Rule 106

What sentence(s) in this rule stands out for you?

How would you define this rule for your social media followers?

God, Abraham, and Sin
HBTQ Rule 107

In the Book of Genesis, you will find passages that the religious right uses to vilify same-gender relationships. In most cases, they point to passages that are untrue. One mythical passage the religious right often quotes is "The city of Sodom was destroyed by God because the city was full of homosexuals." In order to address this particular statement, you must understand the historical context, the customs, the traditions, and the culture of Jewish people at that time. After you have done these things, you are ready to discover why the city was destroyed. The answers are contained within the book of Genesis. Here's what God really said to Abraham:

> "And the Lord said, Because the cry of Sodom and Gomorrah is great, and because their sin is grievous, I will go down now, and see whether they have done altogether according to the cry of it, which is come unto me; and if not I will know (Genesis 1:20–21, KJV).

In the conversations between God and Abraham, the word *homosexual*, or male-to-male relationships, as being against God, are never spoken of as a rationale for the city's destruction. God said that their "sin is grievous." In other words, all the people in the city, including heterosexuals, had little time to focus on God. It is implied that maybe the city dwellers knew a good party when they saw one, and having done so, they paid the ultimate price.

What about this word *homosexual,* and why does it have so much power? God created Adam and Eve—that's it, end of story. Do you accept the statement as true, or does that statement deserve further exploration?

The word *homosexual* comes from the Greek word *homo* meaning *same* and the Latin word *sexualis* meaning *sex*. It's important to understand that the placing of those two words together happened originally in Germany about a hundred years ago . However, it wasn't until the early part of the twentieth century that the USA injected the word into mainstream culture. Somehow around that time, the meaning of the word was highlighted in what's called the New Revised Standard Version Bible (NRSV). The word has been used in many biblical versions since that time. Liberation theologians and biblical scholars on the subject, like Dr. Jeffery Skier, Archbishop Carl Bean, Bishop Zachary Jones, and Dr. John Boswell, all will tell you that the word *homosexuality* is not mentioned in the Ten Commandments. They will tell you that the word is not even mentioned in the Old Testament law books. In the New Testament, the gospels and prophets, including Paul, do not say homosexuality is against God. Even Jesus himself does not discuss the topic of same sex behavior at all. Jesus's central teaching is about God's love for all mankind, and that includes you.

The rules advise you when attending a Christian church and affirming who you are, the King James Version (KJV) of the Bible makes better sense.

As a reminder, the Bibles, written during this last century, have been manipulated by the conservative editors to fit their own interpretation of what they believe God said.

The first argument against same-sex attraction is located in Genesis, the creation story. In other words, the Creation story begins with Adam and Eve. If you believe the story according to all three great religions of the western world, Genesis describes the beginning of mankind. Dr. Jeffery Siker and Dr. Peter Gomes have separately published great literary books and articles about Adam and Eve, addressing sexuality in the creationism story: *The authors of Genesis were intent upon answering the question "where do we come from?" Then, as now the only plausible answer is from the union of a man and a woman. The biological fact is attended by the cultural assumptions of the world in which the writers lived . . . The creation story in Genesis does not pretend to be a history of anthropology or of every social relationship. It does not mention friendship, for example and yet we do not assume that friendship is condemned or abnormal. It does not mention the single state, and yet we know that singleness is not condemned . . . The creation story is not, after all, a paradigm about marriage, but rather about the establishment of human society* (*The Good Book,* Peter Gomes, 1996, and *How to Decide,* Dr. Jeffry Skier, 1994).

Mankind debated same-sex attraction since before the idea of one God existed. The authors of Genesis could only write the creation story one way—through their own worldview. The story of Adam and Eve may have been written to provide instruction about how heterosexual couples should procreate so that the culture survived. The rules remind you that all the major world religions, including Islam, and Christianity, have their foundations in Judaism.. Moreover, both the creation story and Sodom and Gomorrah are described in all three faiths as well.

God, Abraham, and Sin
HBTQ Rule 107

What sentence(s) in this rule stands out for you?

How would you define this rule for your social media followers?

Genesis and Acts of Violence
HTQB Rule 108

The rules encourage you to read the Bible for yourself and without religious instruction filters. By taking this advice, you will understand the historical context concerning the relationship between God, Abraham, and Lot and how it relates to the cities of Sodom and Gomorrah. It is also important to know that when you hear conservatives accuse you of being a sodomite, you should feel confident as you enlighten them with the real truth. The definition is explained like this: Sodomites were the names of the people who were from the town of Sodom, just like people from New York are called New Yorkers, people from Texas are called Texans, or people at the time that were from Canaan were called Canaanites.

Another part of the Sodom and Gomorrah story used against same-sex relationships comes from another chapter in the Book of Genesis:

> *"And they called unto Lot, and said unto him, where are the men who came into thee this night? Bring them out unto us, that we may know them"* (Genesis 19:5, KJV).

Those last words in that verse, "that we may know them," as recent as the early twentieth century, caused the religious right to interpret that verse to mean that the men of Sodom wanted Lot to bring the male angels out so that they could rape them. History teaches you that during this period, with wealthy men like Lot, society dictated that when guests arrived, the affluent took their visitors around town and introduced them to the community.

Lot's knowledge of what was about to happen to the city and the fact that these men were God's messengers led him to feel it was his duty to respect their right to privacy. How those five words at the end of that sentence were interpreted as men having sex with each other is beyond logic.

An interesting fact, overall the nineteenth chapter of Genesis, according to what is postulated by many conservatives discussed the idea of a sexual criminal assault. Rape, which is what the verse refers to is an act of violence conservatives use it to describe lewd behavior between MAMs and it's just not factual. Statistics on the subject states most rape, molestation, and physical abuse cases are committed by the heterosexual population, not the homosexual one.

Genesis and Acts of Violence
HTQB Rule 108

What sentence(s) in this rule stands out for you?

How would you define this rule for your social media followers?

Leviticus and Questions Raised

or

"Thou shall not lie with mankind, as with womankind: it is an abomination" (Leviticus, 18:20, KJV)

HBTQ Rule 109

There is an old saying passed down from generation to generation—"sweep around your own front door before you sweep around mine!" This helpful advice highlights the notion that before you stand in judgment of another, make sure you have taken care of your own issues. Moreover, if you are truly taking care of your own business, you won't have time to concern yourself with others. The Levitical law is based on what some call God's judgment, but the concern is that these laws were written by a few men who were seen as leaders in their community. Since these laws were written by men, one question is, whose judgment is it really?

The rules ask you to read these laws written more than two thousand years ago and unpack the words on the pages of the Old Testament or the Torah. Once you have done so, it will enable you to understand the historical context of this new religious community during that time. The Mosaic Code, otherwise known as the Book of Leviticus, was written for a specific reason, the belief in one God. The ancient Hebrews were surrounded and influenced by other nations, or empires like the Egyptians, the Phoenicians, the Canaanites, and the Aegeans. The Phoenicians, a seafaring society, were considered the ancient trendsetters during the time when the Hebrews were establishing their society and culture.

The Phoenician culture was unique because they not only worshiped many different gods, but it was the men of that culture who were most interesting. These men, who had great influence over the ancient Hebrews, wore long colorful dresses and grew their hair out and bathed in perfumed. Phoenician men applied makeup to their faces, and they even wore elaborate jewelry.

The inference here is that the Hebrew leaders knew these outside cultures, with their pagan worship, sexual experimentation, relations outside of marriage, and dietary consumption, could cause the infant

Hebrew nation to become irrelevant if not addressed. With this fact in mind, the church leaders created laws and separated them into categories. There are two types of laws or codes contained within the Book of Leviticus. One category of laws addressed ritual impurity, and the other basically addressed sexual acts that were considered an abomination. Examples of the ritual impurity include eating shellfish, mixing seeds, wearing fabric that has been woven together, placing marks on your body, eating pork, and working on the Sabbath. The acts of abomination were described as: lying with mankind as with womankind, having sexual relations with in-laws, having sex with friends of your wife, or of course having sexual relations outside of your marriage.

In today's society, many of these laws are not followed, nor are they considered criminal acts in most free nations. If this were true, anyone who has tattoos or body piercings are sinners according to the Book of Leviticus.

Even people who wear jeans or linen or other cotton blends have broken the law. When you eat crabs, shrimps, oysters, lobsters, bacon, roast pork, even if you enjoy Jell-O, you are a sinner according to the law.

Did the church leaders create these laws to protect and preserve their culture because of outside influences?

Why is the law surrounding men who have sex with other men clung to so tightly today by the conservative community?

Is the Book of Leviticus, today, like a buffet, society chooses which ones to follow, and what you don't accept gets thrown away?

Leviticus and Questions Raised

or

"Thou shall not lie with mankind, as with womankind: it is an abomination" (Leviticus, 18:20, KJV)

HBTQ Rule 109

What sentence(s) in this rule stands out for you?

How would you define this rule for your social media followers?

Paul's Real Mission, Worldview, and the Word Effeminate
HBTQ Rule 110

Most people, even MAMs, believe that the New Testament in the Bible strongly denounces homosexuality. Likewise, there are those who will tell you that Jesus, the Book of Acts, and the Book of Revelations made references about homosexual activity. The real deal is that none of these beliefs about the New Testament are based in facts; therefore, they are untrue. Keep in mind: you already know from a previous rule that the words *homosexual, gay* or *same-sex orientation* are modern concepts that did not exist all those years ago. As a matter of fact, there are only three or four passages in the New Testament that remotely concerns itself with what we now call same-sex attraction. Three of these passages are located in two of more than ten epistles or letters from the Apostle Paul. It was the Apostle Paul, along with Simon Peter and James, who were instrumental in establishing Christianity to many people of that era.

In the New Testament, conservatives use the letters from Paul to the Romans, the Corinthians, and Timothy as a way to keep MAMs in the back of society's bus. Let's begin with the most famous and controversial passage found in the Book of Romans.

> *Wherefore God also gave them up to uncleanness, through the lusts of their own hearts, to dishonor their own bodies between themselves: who changed the truth of God into a lie, and worshipped and served the creature more than the Creator, who is blessed forever. Amen. For this cause God to gave them up unto vile affections; for even their women did change the natural use into that which is against nature:*
>
> *And likewise also the men, leaving the natural use of the woman, burned in their lust one toward another; men with men working that which is unseemly, and receiving in themselves that recompense of their error which was meet. And even as they did not like to retain God in their knowledge, God gave them over to a reprobate mind, to do those things, which are not convenient* (Romans 1:24–28, KJV).

To understand this passage in the Bible, you have to consider the source and what the message's purpose was during that era. Paul's writing of this letter and all the rest was to confirm, recruit, and send greetings to the new Christians of the Roman Empire, many of whom at that time was in, what historians would call, morale decline.

When you place the passage in context, you will discover that Paul was thinking about finding and keeping followers for his new church. During that time, he could only depend upon Jewish law he had internalized from the Old Testament. He also relied upon Saul, his a.k.a., before he became a follower of Jesus.

In today's terms, Saul was a bad boy; he stole, he cheated, and he spent time in jail. Therefore, it's safe to conclude that the Apostle Paul knew the streets, in other words he knew what was up. The Apostle Paul had knowledge that the Roman Empire was in the decline; he knew that immorality and lawlessness was a way of life in many early Christian communities within the empire. He also knew there were members of the church who had sexual activities outside of the marriage bedroom. Therefore, it is not a leap to consider that the Apostle Paul wrote the letters to keep the followers of Jesus from straying too far away from the new religion.

> *God also gave them up to uncleanness, through the lusts of their own hearts, to dishonor their own bodies between themselves: men with men working that which is unseemly* (Romans 1:24, KJV).

> *And likewise also the men, leaving the natural use of the woman, burned in their lust one toward another* (Romans 1:27, KJV).

The key phrase of this chapter is men and women are leaving their natural use for each other. Did these statements from Paul imply that he was referring to heterosexuals? Male and female marriage resulting in procreation was all he knew, and when the Apostle Paul saw anything happening outside of this worldview, he addressed these activities in his letters and throughout his travels. For the Apostle Paul, it was natural for people to be attracted to the opposite sex, marry, and have children. When he found out that the flock was involved in, say orgies and wife swapping and any form of sexual expression outside of procreation, they were leaving what Paul described as their natural use for each other.

In addition to his past, Paul was born a Hebrew, and he was also Roman; so it's safe to infer that he knew the empire's indulgence in sexual behavior that was prohibited according to the old law. During the Apostle Paul's era, new Christians were still being influenced by other cultures that held on to their old pagan beliefs. He wanted to address the reality of the time. He wanted new Christians to worship the one true God, and morality was paramount.

When you read these passages in the way Paul intended, these verses make sense. In his worldview, the notion of male-to-male relationships was not considered in his thinking about Christianity. The bottom line is that you can blame this controversy on the rewriting of the Bible in the late nineteenth and early twentieth centuries.

The King James Version of the Bible was revised at that time to speak to a modern audience, and so are Biblical books written in the last century. While an updated Bible can be a good thing, how interesting it is that these editors decided to twist and turn the morality passages into their conservative understanding. This conservative interpretation has influenced all Christian thinking over the past one hundred years; Timothy's letter from Paul is another example of this point.

Passages in the Book of I Timothy has been perverted to include "same-gender attraction" is not exactly accurate. Here is what the Apostle Paul wrote: *But we know that the law is good, if a man use it lawfully; knowing this, that the law is not made for the righteous man, but for the lawless and disobedient, for the ungodly and for sinners, for unholy and profane, for murderers of fathers and murderers of mothers, for manslayers, for whoremongers, for them that defile themselves with mankind, for manstealers, for liars, for perjured persons, and if there be any other thing that is contrary to sound doctrine* (1 Timothy 1:8–10, KJV).

Note that there is no mention of homosexuality because this chapter is all about prostitution. In addition, there are theologians who will tell you that when he heard that the flock was engaging in sex for money, Paul was horrified. With this knowledge in mind, he wrote in 1 Timothy 1:8–10. The verses say if you are doing the right thing according to the old law, then you are safe. If you are sleeping with male and female prostitutes, then both you and the prostitute are breaking the old law. When you are confronted with this passage, as a MAM, push back, explain the chapter. Keep in mind: this verse is speaking about sex for money, so it does not apply to you or your life!

Last but certainly not least is Corinthians, and more than any other book in the Bible, there are two verses that directly speak of a "certain kind of man", or so we're told.

> *Know ye not that the unrighteous shall not inherit the kingdom of God? Be not deceived; neither fornicators, nor idolaters, nor adulterers, nor effeminate, nor abusers of themselves with mankind, nor thieves, nor covetous, nor drunkards, nor revilers, nor extortionists, shall inherit the kingdom of God* (1 Corinthians 6:9–10, KJV).

These verses require you to understand each part of the whole and apply it to what is relevant in today's society. With this in mind, if you believed in the consistency of Paul's letter to this church, then you can't go to heaven if you have premarital sex because you are a fornicator. If you believe in fame, money, and material things above God, then you are one of the idolaters. If you have sex outside your marriage or committed relationship, then you are one of the adulterers. If you pay or get paid for sexual pleasures, then you have become one of the abusers of mankind. If you are hating on others because of what they have, then you are covetous. If you are an alcoholic, cigarette smoker, or use substances, you are one of the drunkards. Finally, if you are one of the party people hanging out in bars and dance clubs, then you have joined the revelers. The question here is: how many individuals you know can meet the bar set by the examples found in Corinthians?

Wait, hold on before we leave this rule. Let's briefly define the term *effeminate,* a powerful word in that biblical chapter. If you apply the meaning of the word *effeminate* as written, Paul was addressing men he assumed were heterosexuals. For the apostle, what this word meant for him was any sexual act not accepted by church leaders and was viewed as something men should not be doing, and therefore, it was a sin.

This passage also begs the question: what kind of "feminine" was Paul referring to?

Is the answer he was addressing men who performed head on women during orgies?

Was he referring to men who did not participate in sporting events? Or men who cooked for their wives? Or husbands who nurtured children? Or was he referring to men who wore makeup like the Babylonians and Egyptians? In all of Paul's letters addressing the morale issues of the day, he repeatedly relied on the old law as a means of foundation.

No matter what the religious right may tell you, to sum up what some Christians say matters to God. All you have to do is look at these self-affirming passages which are so eloquently written in the Book of Matthew:

> *Then the King will say to those at his right hand, Come, you that are blessed by thy Father, inherit the kingdom prepared for you from the foundation of the world; for I was hungry and you gave me food, I was thirsty and you gave me something to drink, I was a stranger and you welcomed me, I was naked and you gave me clothing, I was sick and you took care of me, I was in prison and you visited me.*
>
> *Then the righteous will answer him, Lord when was it that we saw you hungry and gave you food, or thirsty and gave you something to drink? And when was it that we saw you a stranger and welcomed you, or naked and gave you clothing? And when was it that we saw you sick or in prison and visited you? And the King will answer them, Truly I tell you, just as you did it to one of the least of these who are members of our family, you did it unto me.* (Matthew 25:31–40, RSV). Enough said!

Paul's Real Mission, Worldview, and the Word Effeminate
HBTQ Rule 110

What sentence(s) in this rule stands out for you?

How would you define this rule for your social media followers?

The RAB Rules a.k.a. the 800 Series

Congratulations! By reviewing the fifty rules represented in this book, you have begun to create a life road map. As you can see, there are great rewards, as well as great responsibility, in living life as a true liberated man who is attracted to the same sex. There are those of you who will say or think, well, why didn't the rules cover this, or what about that? Some may reject many of the rules that were described and still wonder about their place in this world. *Adam and Steve: The Rules for Men Who Are Attracted to Other Men* believe that if you have to ask yourself these questions, then its job has been done. There are so many rules for men who are attracted to the same sex; just one book could not possibly cover them all.

According to your own experiences, what was not covered?

What are the rules would you add to this book?

The only requirement for submitting rules is that it must be based on facts or solid observations or real experiences, and it must be relatable to a wider audience. The rules you create should be able to fit under the five key categories, like history and the Bible, good living and your power, maturity status, style intimacy and making a connection, or sex and sexuality.

In this chapter, you will find some need-to-know rules. These are postscripts or a prologue of mostly antidotal information that did not get into the preceding chapters. In addition, you will find out about verbal erotic management or VEM. VEM is an all-male discussion group concerning the topics found in this book. Here are the RAB rules, a.k.a. the 800 series.

The 800 Series

RAB Rule 800: The most powerful sex organ you possess is your own brain.

RAB Rule 801: As you mature, you will find that your sexuality is fluid; qualities you are attracted to in this moment will be redefined as you have life experiences.

RAB Rule 802: Clutching your pearls came from classic movies where every time hurt feelings occurred or something shocking happened, one lets out a gasp. It is said that wealthy white women would hold onto the string of pearls hanging around their necks when hit with a notorious surprise. Today, some MAMs mimic this affectation by placing the left or right hand on your throat in a dramatic way. Both hands placed in that position was considered a double clutch of the pearls.

RAB Rule 803: If you own your own home or rent your own apartment, then it is a smart idea not to have random sex with someone from the block or street you live on. If you ignore this rule and have neighborhood trade, then don't be surprised if he violates the boundaries you've set up for visitors to your home.

RAB Rules: 800–803

What sentence(s) in this rule stands out for you?

How would you define this rule for your social media followers?

RAB Rule 804: There is a difference between making love and passionate sex. One concerns itself with a deeper committed connection, and the other has to do with sensual enjoyment for the moment.

RAB Rule 805: In many cases, just because he comes to see you for sex does not mean you are in a romantic relationship with him. The only way he will know your understanding of what the two of you have is if you tell him. Once you have done so, then the chips, as they say, will fall where they may.

RAB Rule 806: The nature of your intimate relationship with another male has to be established and acknowledged by both parties. In other words, one of you cannot make this decision on your own, independent of him..

RAB Rule 807: A fetish is a sexual fantasy that both physically and emotionally turns you on to the point of an erotic appreciation. A fetish is authentic only if it makes you erect and in many cases makes you cum while engaging in the act. Some of the major fetishes enjoyed today include nipple play, foot worshiping, tossing salad, sex toys, and water sports.

RAB Rules: 804–807

What sentence(s) in this rule stands out for you?

How would you define this rule for your social media followers?

RAB Rule 808: One fetish that has come out of the closet recently is called foot worshiping. If you have a foot fetish, then it means there is an erotic feeling that occurs within you—anytime you think about another man's feet. The sexual arousal you have is heightened when socks come off, exposing bare clean, callous and corn-free feet. Classic foot worshiping starts by holding his feet in your hands, bringing them up to your face, and slowly kissing them. This action is a prelude for him to get him comfortable with the different sensations felt while being worshipped. Foot worshipping can be achieved by toe sucking, along with tongue exploration of the entire tibia and fibula. If everything comes together, both of you will have an erection. This is one of the few fetishes that can be performed in foreplay and in the sexual act itself.

RAB Rule 809: Water sports have made a huge comeback in some MAM circles. One aspect of what's considered a water sport is a golden shower. This act includes urinating or being urinated on, resulting in an erection, causing eventual ejaculation. The act of peeing on someone or feeling the warm sensation of a golden shower provides pleasure to many who engage in this activity. If you engage in this fetish, just make sure your partner has agreed to this activity as well. Moreover, keep in mind that ingesting urine is an unhealthy idea. But if this is your thing, the act is best conducted in a bathtub or by placing plastic over the bed.

RAB Rules: 808 and 809

What sentence(s) in this rule stands out for you?

How would you define this rule for your social media followers?

RAB Rule 810: The most popular toys with many MAMs are dildos, anal beads, and flashlight pumps. There is a technique when using these toys; take your time and explore what feels good to you and refer to rule 507B.

RAB Rule 811: Food worship or using food products during the sexual encounter can be exciting. This act is done by placing these items on your naked body while he mostly uses his mouth and tongue for sexual foreplay. But be informed: stay away from using alcohol-based items or citrus on your body. While honey, chocolate syrup, or whipped cream are sexy, make sure he is not allergic. Also, get rid of those items once the act is over. Place a towel on the bed. Enjoy and watch your sheets!

RAB Rule 812: Watching pornography is a healthy act to engage in when you're home alone or even with a partner. Be mindful: if you find yourself needing porn every time you engage in sex, it sends the message that he's unable to arouse you without another visual.

RAB Rule 813: MAMs who participate in pornography have the capacity to engage in a healthy relationship outside of their money-making activity. However, when your sexual acts are recorded, you must be ready for whatever consequences come with public exposure. If you are clear that you are selling a fantasy, then having sex in front of a camera is just another temporary job!

RAB Rules: 810–8013

What sentence (s) in this rule stands out for you?

How would you define this rule for your social media followers?

RAB Rule 814: If you are making money using sex or hustling, then know your worth, know your limitations, and make these instructions clear to the client. If you find yourself getting in touch with the client more than the client is getting in touch with you, then you are hustling backward! Having emotions for a client because he seems always available can be very dicey. Remember: if he is being too generous, too available, then you should question if you are being set up for dependence. Once you become dependent on him, the power in the pay-to-play relationship has shifted to his hands.

RAB Rule 815: Make your own money, pay your own bills, and have your name on the lease or deed.

RAB Rule 816: Be sure you to spend your money wisely and always save at least 3 percent of your salary each payday. During emergency times, throughout life, this advice will come in handy. Even if you spend the savings, replace it using the same formula. When it comes to saving money, as long as you have an income, reestablishing a savings is never a problem!

RAB Rule 817: There are lyrics that said, *if I had a dime, it's yours as well as mine. I'd keep the penny you, know I would, and gladly give you the nine! I can't say no, if he asks me.* The rules say if you only have a dime, then he may have three cents. Never give him more than you would give to yourself!

RAB Rule 818: Love and loyalty cannot be purchased with money—no matter how many coins you have!

RAB Rule 819: If your intention is not just a one-night stand, then try to delay sexual gratification. By doing so, you can get to know him first before you give him your temple, otherwise known as your body, mind, and spirit!

RAB Rules: 804–819

What sentence(s) in this rule stands out for you?

How would you define this rule for your social media followers?

Verbal Erotic Management
(VEM): No. 900

There are many MAMs who may be uncomfortable discussing topics contained within the rules. The author understands how difficult this is for a number of males to express some of those emotions; it depends upon the time and the place. Like for instance, men don't mind having a conversation with each other in a locker room, but most men will not speak to each other while in a public bathroom. VEM challenges each reader attracted to the same sex to engage in this nonsexual, nonthreatening discussion group bearing your body, feelings, opinions, and ideas with others. The objective of VEM is to sit with other adult males, discuss the rules or some aspect about your life while stripped down to your underwear.

The most important guideline of VEM is that you cannot touch yourself or anyone else in the group. A group member may discuss any topic he likes, but absolutely no physical contact can occur while the group is active. By participating in a verbal erotic management group, you display your emotional and body image issues regardless of physique type. By participating in this way, you should also discover that you are not alone.

Here's how it works:

- The group meets quarterly, in other words, every three months. The meetings last for about an hour and a half.
- The group should consist of no less than four and no more than seven men so that everyone has a turn to speak. MAMs must be at least twenty-three years of age and older in order to participate, or the group is not considered a VEM.

- The guidelines postulate that twenty-three is the age when most men are mature enough to verbally process their feelings in an objective manner.
- The members must vote for the group leader or facilitator. It is suggested that you rotate this task because the leader's role is to keep the discussions focused and ensure that everyone participates.
- The leader of the group is the first to remove all of his clothing down to the underwear only. Then one by one, each of the members should take off his garments until everyone is appropriately undressed. The guidelines of VEM state that each of you must agree to take off your clothes in order to participate. No one should ever be fully naked; T-shirts and underwear are required during the group.
- One more time, you cannot touch anyone during group! You may adjust yourself, but you may not touch yourself either.
- There are three elements in the VEM process: including conversation, confrontation, and closure. Conversation means each person is allowed up to three minutes, depending on the size of the group to discuss an issue(s) covered in the book that relates to your day-to-day life where things went well or not so well. Afterward, either you or the leader asks the group for feedback.
- Confrontation means feedback from the group should be given in the positive. There is no yelling, reading, or shady behavior.. Any concerns, as well as criticism should be framed in the form of a question.
- Closure is called by the leader; this is when the individual and the group members sum up the issues presented, if the individual is satisfied. The topic ends, and the next person is selected. The process starts again.
- The goal is for each person to feel a sense of being a part something larger than the individual by having shared with the group. VEM could enable you to raise your confidence level around others. Also, VEM will help you become more assertive concerning educational pursuits and career directions. If you can come from a deep place while almost naked, then expressing yourself outside of the group to get what you want is almost assured.

Verbal Erotic Management
(VEM): No. 900

What sentence(s) in this rule stands out for you?

How would you define this rule for your social media followers?

Name five males you would invite to a VEM that you host.

The Rules in Texts and Tweets

The Golden Rule No. 1: Men who are attracted to other men (MAM) can replace the term *gay*. Not all MAMs express themselves in identical ways.

HB Rule 100: Same-sex attraction has been a part of the human experience since the evolution of man.

HB Rule 100B: Bullies have a negative impact in the young lives of MAMs.

HB Rule 101: Your nature is not a lifestyle choice. It's a different life, which is just as valuable as any heterosexuals'.

HB Rule 101B: Your same-sex attraction is your natural birthright; you had no choice in the matter.

HB Rule 102: Before you were born, your blessing in life was to be attracted to the same sex.

HB Rule 102B: Genetics, environment, and hormonal factors influence birth.

HB Rule 103: In the animal kingdom, several hundred species engage in same-sex attraction.

HB Rule 103B: In all the major ancient societies and cultures, male pairing prior to marriage was a part of the fabric of life.

HB Rule 104: There are three examples of same sex situations within the Bible.

HB Rule 104B: In the Book of I Samuel, you will find a love story about two men.

HB Rule 105: Present-day homophobia can find its roots in the Torah, the Bible, and the Quran.

HB Rule 106: The rules state that for a MAM, the key to biblical interpretation means understanding the words for yourself.

HB Rule 106B: It has been documented that King James I sexual appetites surpassed his cousin Queen Elizabeth I featuring young men at court .

HB Rule 107: The word *homosexual* was added to our culture during the early twentieth century with the introduction of the RSV of the Bible. . .

HB Rule 107B: The story of Adam and Eve may have been written to provide instruction about how heterosexuals should sex each other.

HB Rule 108: Sodomites was a name of a group of people who were from the town of Sodom, just like people from Texas are called Texans.

HB Rule 109: If the Levitical laws were written by man. One question is: whose judgment is it really?

HB Rule 109B: There are two types of laws contained in the Book of Leviticus. One category is ritual impurity, and the other isbasically sexual acts. .

HB Rule 110: In the New Testament, conservatives use the letters from the Apostle Paul as a way to keep MAMs in the back of society's bus.

GLP Rule 200: It is a universal truth that your same sex biology is all nature.

GLP Rule 201: Reparative therapy has been debunked by all the major mental health associations in the USA.

GLP Rule 201B: The notion that you could be conditioned to same-sex attraction or someone can turn you out is an assumption that's not based on facts.

GLP Rule 202: There are vested or authentic authority. Which definition fits you?

GLP Rule 202B: Bayard Rustin was not only brilliant but a proud and unashamed MAM.

GLP Rule 203: When you are living your truth, you have internalized who you are.

GLP Rule 204: According to the rules, there is a talent in you; use it because it is an expression of your internal creation.

GLP Rules 204B: James Baldwin used his talents to accomplish many goals during his lifetime despite homophobia and racism.

GLP Rule 205: One of the most common yet nonproductive emotions you can have is anger.

GLP Rule 205B: Oscar Wilde allowed negative emotions to control his rational thought.

GLP Rule206: The rules concerning coming out or revealing your MAM nature is that it's not a one-time process.

GLP Rule 206B: Back in the 1930s, 1940s, and 1950s, during George Cukor became the unofficial host of Hollywood same-sex cultural elite.

GLP Rule 207: Never allow anyone to judge you because of whom you are attracted to or who you have in your bed.

GLP Rule 208: You must heal and validate your own spirit on a frequent basis. By doing so, you free yourself from needing other's approval.

GLP Rule 208B: It is to be expected that as the years go by and each of you mature, not everyone in your circle of friends will stay close to each other.

GLP Rule 209: There is a universal path that will lead you to greatness, and this is achieved after you find peace in the life you've chosen for yourself.

GLP Rule 209B: Start beliving that self actualization or greatness can be achieve in the first place ..

GLP Rule 210: As an MAM, you should always strive to improve your emotional and intellectual well-being.

GLP Rule 210B: Sylvester was a MAM musical artist who helped introduced the androgynous and drag persona to the public.

MS Rule 300: The rules identify five stages of maturity, namely the neophytes, ingénues, supernovas, ikonoclass, and legacies.

MS Rule 301: Neophyte comes from the Greek word meaning new; this occurs before age twelve until your late teens.

MS Rule 302: Neophytes are learning how to express themselves; some will do it overtly, and other will take a subtle approach.

MS Rule 303: Parents and other family members must be supportive of a neophyte's self-expression or face the consequences of doing nothing.

MS Rule 304: The neophyte stage is the time when you begin to shape your likes and dislikes according to your individual personality.

MS Rule 305: The term *ingénue* is a French word used to describe an adult who is young and new. It occurs between young adulthood and ends during your early thirties.

MS Rule 306: The ingénue stage is about the realization that you are legally responsible for your own life's path.

MS Rule 307: The supernova stage happens from early thirties to the midforties. When you've reached this stage, you are old enough to have made a past.

MS Rule 308: The ikonoclass stage happens from the mid- to late forties until around your early sixties; in this stage, you are in a rarefied category.

MS Rule 309: The legacy stage happens from midsixties and beyond. More than any other generation, you have the most experience with change.

MS Rule 310: In most cases, each generation seeks relationships or sexual gratification by choosing peers within eight years of their age group. Some don't!

SIMC Rule 400: When first meeting another man, in many cases, he has to be physically appealing to you and only you.

SIMC Rule 400B: Who you are attracted to or what turns you on is an individual choice.

SIMC Rule 401: If you are a man attracted to the same sex, then you have a conscious sense of your own unique swagger, style, and elegance.

SIMC Rule 402: Calling where you live home or your villa is a serious declaration about who you are and what you are about.

SIMC Rule 402B: As a MAM, your home is a reflection of your personality, representing the real side of you.

SIMC Rule 403: The terms *reading, shade,* and *trade* all have different meanings, depending on how you use them.

SIMC Rule 404: Substance use can make you become psychologically and physically dependant.

SIMC Rule 404B: If you have sexual addiction, then you make the act of sex a priority in your life.

SIMC Rule 405: Being crafty or pulling a stunt simply means engaging in illegal or mischievous behaviors which can lead to criminal prosecution.

SIMC Rule 406: As a drag or tranny, you are a part of the MAM spectrum because you have in common with other men who are attracted to the same sex.

SIMC Rule 407: A MITCH is a bisexual who derives sexual pleasure by enjoying role play with drag queens or trannys.

SIMC Rule 407B: The average bisexual is a MAM who enjoys the social and sexual pleasures of both males and females.

SIMC Rule 407C: An MCM is a heterosexual male who is secure in his manhood; he has no judgment about you.

SIMC Rule 407D: The May-dar factor is an internal compass so powerful that you could recognized when a stranger is attracted to the same sex.

SIMC Rule 408: Each committed relationship looks different. MAMs establish an unwritten contract with each other.

SICM Rule 408B: Once you've achieved marriage equality, think about how your marriage ceremony should look differently.

SICM Rule 408C: Relationships end long before the physical act of leaving occurs.

SICM Rule 409: The term *online dating* for men who are attracted to the same sex at times can be an oxymoron.

SIMC Rule 409B: Cruising occurs when anytime you begin to use body language as a means of same-sex communication.

SIMC Rule 409C: Contained within this country, from small towns to big cities, rambles and tea rooms exist.

SIMC Rule 409D: There is a myth that MAMs are only attracted to almost perfect beauty and chiseled physiques.

SIMC Rule 410: Men who are attracted to the same sex continue to dominate and influence pop culture genres today.

SIMC Rule 410B: Sports participation both in the stands and as a player are natural events for MAMs to find competitive comfort just like their heterosexual counterparts . .

SS Rule 500: The first thing to understand is, just because you are a MAM does not mean you are defined by how much sex you can engage in.

SS Rule 500B: Copulation is important, but intimacy, companionship, and friendship are even more crucial.

SS Rule 501: The penis is an external male phenomenon that has three parts.

SS Rule 502: One of the most frequent enjoyed sexual activities for a MAM is fellatio.

SS Rule 503: The gluteus maximus or booty is the largest of three muscles located on the back of a human's body.

SS Rule 504: The skill of analingus or rimming or tossing salad is another highly developed art form perfected by MAMs.

SS Rule 505: In the male psyche, sex and intimacy can be one in the same, or it can mean two different things.

SS Rule 505B: Male-to-male intercourse or the act of copulation or fucking has been described as the true physical intimacy.

SS Rule 506: MAMs popularize three basic sexual roles as either top, bottom, or versatile.

SS Rule 507: Frottage is the name given when men are sexually intimate with each other, without penetration.

SS Rule 508: Forms of engagements like threesomes, orgies, and sex parties are as old as mankind.

SS Rule 509: The sadomasochists believe pain and pleasure are the epitome of sexual liberation.

SS Rule 509B: Raw sex or bareback for MAMs means having anal intercourse without condoms.

SS Rule 509C: Breeding or seeding happens when, while having raw sex, you ejaculate inside the anus.

SS Rule 510: Sexually transmitted diseases or STDs have been affecting mankind for as long as there has been civilized society.

SS Rule 510B: According to medical facts, STDs are classified either as a disease that affects the genitals or a viral infection.

The MAM Anthem (I)

I am quicksilver, a fleeting shadow, and a distant sound;
My home has no boundaries beyond in which I cannot pass;
I live in a flash of color, in music, in fashion, in finance, in sports, and in the great works of art;
I live on the wind, in the sparkle of a star, I am his son, and I am her son, the chosen one;
I am a man who is attracted to other men!

Edited by: Russell Baptist

www.ingramcontent.com/pod-product-compliance
Lightning Source LLC
Chambersburg PA
CBHW020455030426
42337CB00011B/122